THE WHITE STONE

THE WHITE STONE

STONE

The Art of Letting Go

Esther de Waal

LITURGICAL PRESS
Collegeville, Minnesota

www.litpress.org

Copyright © 2021 Esther de Waal
Originally published in the UK under the title
The White Stone
by the Canterbury Press,
an imprint of Hymns Ancient & Modern Ltd of
13a Hellesdon Park Road, Norwich, Norfolk NR6 5DR

Published in the United States of America by
Liturgical Press, Collegeville, Minnesota 56321

Library of Congress Cataloging-in-Publication data available

ISBN 978-0-8146-6789-7

for
Theo and Emmy

This small book is a direct outcome of the months spent in lockdown as a result of the pandemic of the years 2020–21. It is highly personal, a long conversation with myself that those weeks of solitude encouraged. Writing has always been for me a means of exploring my feelings, making sense of my situation. So, I picked up my pen and began to write what became a monologue, as I looked back to the leaving of a place in the Welsh Marches that had meant so much to me over many years, and my arrival in my new home Oxford.

We all have to face up to the process of letting go at intervals throughout our lives, and for everyone the response will be very different. I feel that what I have achieved amounts to little more than hints and glimpses into a vast and vital topic. I hope that this book may encourage others to dialogue with what I have written here.

I owe a deep debt of gratitude to my family for the practical help and moral support over recent years. Among the friends whose stalwart presence has meant much is Claudia Wald. And a very warm mention must go to Pegasus Grange in Oxford and the generosity of its welcome to me.

E de W
20 August 2021
The Feast of St Bernard

Apologia

I slip my hand into my pocket to check if it is still there – just a small white stone. I feel its rough edge but I do not need to pull it out, I just need to have the reassurance of its presence. I am walking along a crowded pavement in a busy city, which is at once beautiful and alien. These buildings speak a language new to me – no longer the vernacular of cottages and barns, simple, humble churches, small muddy lanes. Here instead one magnificent view succeeds another; this is a city of grand vistas, speaking of the pursuit of wisdom, the search for beauty. William Wordsworth loved its High Street, praising 'the stream-like windings of that glorious street'. Christopher Wren left his mark on the place, as did Nicholas Hawksmoor and many other illustrious names. But there are also the more intimate glimpses, small streets called Turnagain Lane or Catte Street. There are forgotten graves in an out-of-the-way cemetery where one can pay homage to some of the noble figures of university life. The college chapels house incomparable treasures, not least in their stained-glass windows. I am just beginning to learn the roll call of names of the men and women blessed in holiness or learned in scholarship who are remembered here, from the Saxon St Frideswide to the Victorian Lewis Carroll. Each walk I take shows me something new. Every time I come into the city I pass a memorial to Lord Nuffield and I remember that St Aldates was the old Jewish quarter.

There is so much to discover. I am glad that Jan Morris (who was a chorister at Christ Church) should call it 'partly an ark, partly an argosy. Oxford is like a huge wayward cargo of treasures, shipped home by some eccentric entrepreneur with an eye for a promising talent, plenty of money and stubborn preferences of his own.' She allows me to show a little disrespect, which I find reassuring, when she writes: 'As for the nightmare heads outside the Sheldonian Theatre, it is a moot point whether they represent philosophers, Roman emperors or the 12 apostles.' Yet she writes eloquently of that powerful Epstein figure of Lazarus in the ante-chapel of New College, the risen Lazarus still shrouded for the grave, white and tortured, the most haunting statue in Oxford.[1]

I am pleased to see that the Oxford ragwort, or at least a cousin, flourishes on the banks of the rivers Cherwell and Thames, rampant and untidy, bold and splendid, as though making its protest against anything with a hint of grandeur – its Latin name after all is *senecio squalidus*. Its career began here in the seventeenth century when it was imported from either Greece or Sicily, but it escaped and with a preference for gravel or unkempt ground it made its way along the clinker ash of the railway tracks. I find this an enjoyable story. It clambers through some rusty railings on Folly Bridge and the bright yellow catches my eye. Just as I stop there, gazing down at the Thames churning after last night's heavy rain, I hear the sound of Great Tom booming out from Christ Church, mingling with those other chimes of Merton and Magdalen as they succeed one another. I think of the opening lines of Gerard Manley Hopkins:

Duns Scotus's Oxford

Towery city and branchy between towers;
   Cuckoo-echoing, bell-swarmed, lark-charmed,
     rook-racked, river-rounded;[2]

It was written when he was in Oxford in March 1879 (not when he was an undergraduate at Balliol). And that then reminds me of Jude, in Thomas Hardy's *Jude the Obscure*, as a young man gazing at the distant city of Christminster when suddenly the wind reaches him and seems like a message from the place: 'Surely it was the sound of bells, the voice of the city, faint and musical, calling to him, "We are happy here!"'[3]

The stone is still there – I check it once again, remembering its origins in a tiny brook in Herefordshire and contrasting it to the majestic Thames. I walk slowly over Folly Bridge wondering about the Franciscan friar Roger Bacon, a leading light of Oxford's thirteenth-century intellectual life – was his study really here, in a tower on the bridge? I do not know but I shall find out – at the moment, if myth and fact mingle, I can reassure myself that I have time and opportunity to explore the reality of my new landscape.

The Cottage I

The cottage nestles into the side of a gently sloping hill, it looks as though it is naturally a part of the landscape, not imposed upon it. Its name is Cwm, the Welsh word for a shallow valley. The map of this area of the Welsh Marches shows a scattering of *cwms*, as common as the local quarries, and this cottage is built of the local Herefordshire red sandstone as are all the nearby farms and barns. My first memory of it is that it was just like a small child's drawing of the perfect house: square, with four windows and two squat chimneys and a porch over the front door. It felt simple and safe, and the great old yew tree growing on one side seemed to bring a sense of timelessness.

Leonard Woolf wrote in his autobiography *Beginning Again* that, in his experience, 'What cuts the deepest channels in our lives are the different houses in which we live.'[4] He claims that the house, both in its material and its spiritual environment, has an immense influence upon its inhabitants. In his autobiography *Downhill All the Way*,[5] he called one house, in which he and Virginia had lived for twelve years, the most powerful moulder of their lives. It is true: houses shape people, and in return people shape their houses. For houses have a life force. They offer more than shelter: they offer security, stability, a sense of sanctuary.[6] This cottage has brought me that stability, for it has been a continuing presence in my life for over fifty years. Everything about it is familiar and loved. I open the door and go into the kitchen with its red-brown tiles and the kettle singing on the stove. It is a sunny day and the light pours in and plays on the whitewashed walls. The wood of the scrubbed table, the splendid old oak dresser, the shelf of books, the chest for toys, all bring their security, a sense of belonging here – welcoming me in. May Sarton, the American novelist and poet, writes about the 'dear familiar gods of home' and the happiness that is daily being woven into a house:

> And how it is not sudden and it is not given
> But is creation itself like the growth of a tree.
>
> ...
>
> The air is charged with blessing and does bless;
> Windows look out on mountains and the walls are kind.[7]

It is here in this kitchen that I do my writing. The cottage has been enlarged over the years, and there is now a spacious kitchen which has become the centre of the house. Sitting at the kitchen table and at a loss to find the right word, I have only to glance into the garden through the glass-panelled door and gain inspiration from the old wild plum tree, gnarled and moss covered, and beyond that the silver birch, tall and elegant, standing over the graves of the family cats. 'My desk faces the birch tree and the birch tree faces God. I try to get my words in their alignment.'[8] I love what Christian Bobin says, for poetic language is needed to touch the ultimate poetic depths of a house.

Houses are so much more than the bricks and mortar of which they are constructed. A house is our first universe, a real cosmos in every sense of the word, our vital space where we take root, day by day, in a corner of the world. In *The Poetics of Space* Gaston Bachelard shows us that people need houses in order to dream, in order to imagine: 'the house shelters day dreaming, the house protects the dreamer ...'[9] A well-rooted house must be a part of the surrounding location – open to the sound of leaves in the wind, sensitive to the movement of the moon and sun, and to the presence of water. With the door open I can hear the sound of the stream which runs at the end of the garden, and then becomes a waterfall, plunging down on to the rocks below. It was like a living presence, a vital part of living here. And often a verse from the first psalm would run through my head:

> like a tree planted by streams of water,
> bearing fruit in due season,
> with leaves that do not wither.

This is where I belong. I ask myself if I would have been a different person had I grown up with the harsh Aberdeen granite in the countryside of my Scottish forebears, and not the soft red sandstone of the Welsh Borders. The land speaks, and speaks differently according to its terrain. I think of W. H. Auden who wrote so lyrically in praise of limestone, or Paul Nash whose painting was influenced by chalk downs, or Ivor Gurney for whom Gloucestershire was his lifeblood. I think of Laurie Lee returning to Slad to live out his later years in the place of his boyhood, and the headstone to his grave reads: 'He lies in the valley he loved.' I think of what place meant to Edward Thomas ... the string of names could go on and on, listing the poets, writers and painters shaped by their native landscape.

Place matters, and in a time of pandemic as never before. People write about the importance of home, discovering that there is much to celebrate in a home-centred existence. Christianity has long recognized that a sense of place is integral to becoming whole and healthy human beings.[10] Place is the fabric of our lives; memory and identity are stitched through it. It is not to be underestimated: every living creature needs a home, and that home is an expression of what it means for it to be alive. I like the way in which the Dominican Timothy Radciffe tells us that we are 'topophilic' – we all need places in which we may be planted and flourish.[11] Social anthropologists understand this and tell us that the house holds powerful social, symbolic and ritual significance. It is seen variously as a microcosm, an organic whole, even as an animate being, says Renée Hirschon: 'houses and their inhabitants are part of one process of living'.[12] Houses are far from being merely static structures. They are even imaged in terms of the human body and vice versa. An old Indian proverb visualizes each of us as a house with four rooms, a physical, a mental, an emotional and a spiritual, and unless we visit every room daily – even if it is only to keep it aired – we are not a complete person. It is not surprising that for the displaced and the exile there exists a deep and lasting longing for home, which Renée Hirschon calls enduring and pervasive, a longing which remains perhaps the most significant factor of their lives.

I know how much my own personhood is indissolubly bound up with the places in which I have lived. Looking back on my life, I see it as divided into periods dictated not by school, university, marriage and so on, but by place, and more specifically by houses. When I count them up (omitting the house in which I was born and of which I have no recollection) the total comes to seven – and I include a half, for the winters spent in the Cathedral College in Washington DC. It is rather surprising to find that out of that number one only was of my own personal choosing. Of course I did not choose my childhood home, which was a Shropshire vicarage, the 'tied cottage' that went with my father's work as a parish priest. Then when I married a priest, apart from the flat that we rented for the first three years of our married life, I lived successively in different houses dictated first by my own work and then by my husband's ecclesiastical position. Embarking on each new house asked of me energy and imagination – it was like the dialogue with a garden, making it my own yet also respecting its right to be what it naturally was. Each carried its own significance, and had its role in moulding my life. In time I made each one a home that I came to love, and then in turn each one had to be relinquished, no longer mine. And each time that was not of my choosing. And each time it became the occasion of grieving, and a struggle with letting go.

One place, however, stands apart from the rest, and that is the cottage. It was not chosen by us, but it was given – an unexpected and wonderful gift, one for which we were to be eternally grateful. Here was a place that was permanent, on which we could depend, always awaiting our return, always there to welcome us, whatever we had been doing, wherever we had been. It was like the ground base to all our journeying. Penelope Fitzgerald describes it exactly in a phrase that comes in her novel *The Blue Flower* when she writes of 'the sense in that misty valley of relaxation, of perpetual forgiveness, of coming home after one has done one's best'.[13] It came into our life in a most fortuitous way. My sister had bought a mill in Rowlestone in Herefordshire, in the Welsh Marches, in a small hidden valley, which lay down a steep track. My father, finding that the cottage at the top of the track was for sale, set out to see it on a snowy day in February 1967. He immediately bought it and then presented it to us. We could take possession on Lady Day, 25 March – the countryside still observed the old calendar for the exchange of houses. So began the saga that was to run for fifty years.

It was then the traditional two up and two down with a kitchen at the back, and a boxed-in stairway dividing the rooms. The privy was in a small shed with a faded blue door below the yew tree, next to the remnants of an old forge. Built of local stone, it all harmonized naturally with the landscape. It was perfect for the family with four sons that we had by then become. We all fitted in beautifully, the boys in bunk beds, and the house furnished with bargain buys from the local auction. Although the road ran alongside us, traffic was so rare that there would be a rush to the gate to greet anything that passed. The garden faced south and in the coming years we planted masses of daffodils, and my father created an orchard. The previous owners had built a sturdy swing, set in concrete, which meant that we could all swing. I devised long runic chants as I pushed the boys: telling each one in turn how great and glorious they were. That wonderful timeless act of swinging caught something of the rhythm of our life there in those early days, dictated by the light and by the seasons, and by our closeness to the elements. The sun rose over the hill of the Seraphim, and in the evening it fell down behind an outlier of Merlin's mountain. We were inserted – although we would not have articulated it as such – between a world of angels and a world of mythology. This was the Welsh Marches, and there was something timeless and magical about it.

And we were never apart from the sound of water. At one end of the garden two small streams met and fell over a shallow weir, and made a pool, and then they flowed together until they plunged over a waterfall, dashing on to the rocks below. The sound was never the same – it changed endlessly with all its different moods, light and delicate when the water was low, surging and powerful at times of flood. The river was a living presence, of which we were continually aware.

We came here as often as we could, for vacations and long summer holidays, and over the years the cottage responded to our developing needs. As the boys grew and we wanted more people to come and stay we built on the large kitchen with a Rayburn, where we could all congregate. We added a wooden spiral staircase (which for many years I used as a precarious filing system) with a glass wall which ran from floor to ceiling, so that the sun flooded the house. The ruined forge was transformed, and for some time became the workshop for a potter son. The family grew, there were flocks of grandchildren. Sometimes in its life the cottage would be overflowing; in later years I was there on my own. But, growing older, I could not live there alone for ever. The letting go of the cottage after nearly fifty years is the reason that I am writing this – in the first place as solace for myself.

I think of writers who understand attachment to a house. William Fiennes grew up in a medieval moated house that had belonged to his family for generations, and his feeling for it is a thread running through *The Music*

Room. There is a small incident in the book which tells us what the house means to him. He is climbing on the roof when a tile cracks under his foot, exposing the tile underneath to the air for the first time in four hundred years. 'I looked at the sudden bareness with a stab of remorse, not because I fear reprimand or punishment, but because of some idea that I had that the house was a sentient being, vulnerable to injury.'[14] The house is greater than them. One afternoon William had watched his father standing motionless, his palm pressed flat against a buttress. When he asked him what he was doing his father replied that he was asking the house for some of its strength.[15] For a house has its own persona, for good or ill. In Marilynne Robinson's novel *Home*, the house itself, the presbytery of the retired Calvinist minister, plays an important role in the story of the homecoming of the prodigal son. The old man loves it, particularly after the death of his wife when he would speak about it as though it were itself an old wife, beautiful for every grace that it had offered through all those long years. The reality was that 'nothing about that house ever did change, except to fade or scar or wear. Miracles of thrift in their grandparents' generation blessed the stodginess and the shabbiness. All that big, crowding furniture and all that prim and doubtful taste commemorated heroic discipline and foresight.' After any calamity the daughter would fill the house with the smell of cooking, which would mean 'this house has a soul that loves us all, no matter what'.[16] Renée Hirschon sees 'the enduring and pervasive longing for home' as being a most significant factor in the experience of displacement, of those who are long-term exiles from home.[17]

I sit at the kitchen table drawing the house around me like some cloak. But my mind is straying to the garden, the orchard, the copse, the waterfall. Leaving these will be quite as painful as leaving the house itself. You cannot separate a house like this from its natural surroundings. Sound matters, so I go first to stand at the top of the waterfall whose sound has been my constant companion all these past years. To live beside water has the quality of constant change and yet changelessness. I know it so well. I have walked the upper reaches to the source of the two small streams which meet here. To walk in water is very different from following a river along its bank – a stream can be cunning in carving out a path, curving and cutting into the bank, so that it becomes precarious with sudden holes and hazards, rockfalls and fallen trees to scramble over. But there are mosses and liverworts on the banks, beautiful and tactile, and occasionally a rare wild flower whose location must be kept secret. This is a private, mysterious world. When the water is clear the riverbed is a treasury of stones fashioned by the flow into rounded, smooth shapes. This is where I found the white stone.

Living beside water means living with unpredictability. But then nothing in this garden is sure or certain. There are no trim herbaceous borders, no vegetables in careful rows. Instead I think of it as a naturalist's garden. I treat it very much as I would a conversation with an old friend, with much listening and long silences. I have tried to respect and enhance what the land itself is saying. I try not to dominate. It is a partnership which changes all the time, and in which I hope that the land will find its voice. So I clear the brambles and get rid of the thorny undergrowth on the steep riverbanks. It was hard work and I was glad that I knew well a medieval stained-glass window in Canterbury Cathedral, which depicted Adam, naked to the waist, at work, tilling the earth, with an adze hanging in the branch of the tree beside him. I think of him working, with sweat on his face, struggling with really terrible ground.[18] For many of the contemporary viewers, the monastic aphorism *ora et labora* would immediately spring to mind, prayer and work go together. I ask myself if I am trying to create a garden of Eden here, using the equivalent of an adze, removing the destructive forces, letting in the light.

The orchard flourishes – a mass of beautiful blossom in the spring, and in the autumn there will be a plenteous crop of apples from the trees that my father planted. When St Swithun's Day is past and the seeds of flowers have dropped it is the time to cut the grass. An old friend comes with his scythe and I watch the time-honoured sight of the quiet, rhythmic blade at work, almost as though it is whispering gently to the stalks that it is about to cut. In the copse at the edge of the orchard is a clump of trees with two magnificent wild cherries. When they are in bloom the lines of A. E. Housman's poem run through my head – lines that I have known since my Shropshire childhood:

Loveliest of trees, the cherry now
Is hung with bloom along the bough,
…
About the woodlands I will go
To see the cherry hung with snow.[19]

But there is also one dead tree there; it stands sentinel, a little to the side, so that its outline is gaunt, making a stark skeleton against the skyline. I have left it like that on purpose. I had been reading David Jones' *In Parenthesis*, with its dark picture of war and destruction, with its torn trees and the slaughter at Mametz wood, and I wanted to have a reminder in an idyllic garden of just how costly that had been. I did not want a natural world that was prettified, and shorn of pain and disfigurement, in which, as Philip Toynbee wrote, 'there is no room for blood and bone. If we fail to take the pain of creation seriously then we also fail to take the reality of God seriously.'[20]

The wild flowers now come of their own accord since my clearing has brought light and space. The bluebells crowd the steep riverbanks after I got rid of a tangle of brambles and a barrage of thorns, and they share their territory with numerous ferns, and the occasional red campion. But first in the year come the snowdrops, sometimes sheltering under the hedgerows, sometimes spreading out in drifts. In the orchard our Lady's smock is always there in time for Lady Day, 25 March. There are streams of cowslips, together with the buttercups turning the orchard into a cloth of gold. I love the moon daisies when they come, and think of what Bobin said: 'No philosophy under the sun can rival a single ox-eye daisy conversing with the sun, and laughing, laughing, laughing.'[21] There is something essentially joyous about these flowers cascading in their freedom. I cherish the dandelion with its petals of burnished gold quite ravishingly beautiful, and then when it is over there is such an amazing clock of spun lightness. A final accolade, since this list could become far too long, goes to the cow parsley, common everywhere says the Revd Keble Martin rather dismissively in his beautifully illustrated British flora.[22] He is right of course but I wonder if we would pay it more attention if we were to call it by its North American name of Queen Anne's lace – a piece of eighteenth-century gentrification on the part of some early settler? The idea of lace certainly does justice to its wildly profuse rays, which break any rules of geometrical conformity and yet manage to achieve a picture of overall harmony. The blooms, clusters of tiny flowers, have an ethereal quality about them. I like to think of the flower heads as a parasol or an inverted chandelier. And then when the florets die we are left with seed heads that are jolly little black ovals dancing untidily.

This needs a magnifying glass. Only then is it possible to appreciate the pattern and the symmetry, or lack of symmetry, in a flower. Looking at something in this way does not take away the mystery: quite the contrary, it enhances it.[23] This is even more so when I am looking at the grasses in the garden. It is only too easy to take them for granted, but they are delicate, exquisite, and have an enchanting quality about them. Walt Whitman said of them: 'I believe a leaf of grass is no less perfect than the journey-work of the stars.'[24] I have more than once set out to try to learn to differentiate them with the help of Keble Martin and his incomparable illustrations, but I soon abandoned it in favour of simply taking delight in their names – wood mellick, creeping twitch and bearded twitch, rough dog's tail, cocksfoot. Watching how their heads move in a gentle breeze and enjoying their quietly muted colours is reward enough.

The Cottage II

The cottage has always been there, the rock on which I build, to use a phrase from the psalms. It was the place from which I came and went. The children grew and left. A marriage came to an end. I wrote books and I travelled widely. I gave lectures, retreats, quiet days. And always it was there awaiting my return. It grounded me. 'I need to come back to mud, sheep and reality,' as I put it in a letter to my sister as I returned from one of my long journeys. But I am starting to refuse invitations, and as though in response, the invitations fall in number. I travel less. This is the gentle coming to an end of an era. I am getting older. I struggle with some of the heavier work in the garden. I have to accept the fact that soon I will have to leave the cottage. I realize that the time has come when I must relinquish a place that I have deeply loved for fifty years, a place that has helped to make me into the person that I am.

As I begin to think about it I discover that one of the things that happens at a time of leaving – whether a place or a person – is a sharpening of perception. It is as though seeing for the last time is akin to seeing for the first time: it is an urgent, fresh vision. I can take nothing for granted, for it is gift, and I find myself gazing in wonder at whatever is there in front of me. Denise Levertov gives the significant title 'Living' to the poem whose theme is 'last':

> The fire in leaf and grass
> so green it seems
> each summer the last summer.
>
> The wind blowing, the leaves
> shivering in the sun,
> each day the last day.
> ...
> Each minute the last minute.[25]

I need poetry now more than ever – a poetic language that is precise, honed in poems that have short memorable lines that I can easily remember. Poetry knows how to deal with the grief that I keep to myself. It would not be seemly to parade it openly when the future that lies in front of me promises so much. And yet I can only appropriate the next step if I go through a process of grieving for what I am losing:

> Grief, have I denied thee?
> Grief, I have denied thee.

These lines and the following are from Denise Levertov's poem 'A Lamentation'.

> Always denial. Grief in the morning, washed away
> in coffee, crumbled to a dozen errands between
> busy fingers.[26]

Brushing away the pain with busyness – that is a danger. That is why I want quite consciously to stare grief in the face. Perhaps some people would say that it is absurd to feel so strongly about the loss of place. But I feel that this process of embracing this grief is justified, for a home becomes an extension of the self.

How to Grieve

> Stare it in the mangled face.
> Do not turn away
> or accept facile distraction.
> Do not allow words
> to be imposed on you,
> platitudes of hope
> dispensed like spiritual aspirin
> by those who have not been there.[27]

Bonnie Thurston knows that there are no shortcuts in the grieving process. It is simply a matter of time until eventually blessing may embrace the wound.

The Beatitudes tell us:

> How blest are the sorrowful;
> they shall find consolation. (Matthew 5.4)

I love the word 'consolation': it is so strong, it holds out the promise that ultimately God will accomplish a miracle, and we shall be delivered from this time of pain. Here I find that I am being given permission not to deny my feelings. Grieving is part of being human.

It is now late spring, and I have decided to do something intentional with the time remaining before I leave. I have set myself a conscious exercise in visiting the immediate neighbourhood of the cottage for the last time in a deliberately symbolic walk. After all, there is that familiar aphorism of St Augustine, *solvitur ambulando*, it is solved by walking. I shall make it a ritual of leave-taking: I am going to undertake a ritual walk. Different losses might evoke a quite different response. Walking is my way. I need a rite of passage that will mark the ending of the old and the opening up of the new. In the past, such rites would have been common enough, but they have largely disappeared today, to our loss. As Renée Hirschon has said in her lecture 'Dealing with Death': 'Rites of passage are designed to aid the transition and emotional turmoil that occurs at specific points in the life cycle of the human person.' They allow the passage from one stage of life to another, and help to deal smoothly with change. She shows us the rich tradition of the Greek Orthodox in dealing with death, the traditional wisdom accumulated over long years, compared to its absence in much of contemporary life. I am not dealing with a human death, but with the ending of a way of life; I need to celebrate it and to let go.

Since this land has been my mentor, which slowly over the years I have learnt to read, I intend to make the starting point for my ritual a short walk in the immediate area around the cottage, to locations that are familiar and significant to me. The following of a path has about it a timeless quality. 'Children need paths to explore,' says Bruce Chatwin at the start of his book of photographs, *Winding Paths*, 'to take bearings on the earth on which they live, as a navigator takes bearings on familiar landmarks.'[28] Robert MacFarlane has, more than anyone, shown that walking is still profoundly and widely alive as a vital means for people to make sense of themselves – or, as he says, 'to seek joy or encounter grace'.[29] I have found that there is a relationship between walking, thinking and writing, particularly in times of sorrow or sadness. Walking was one of the few activities that could lift Edward Thomas from the depression that dogged his life, and he must have walked thousands of miles along pathways. If I choose to walk I do no more than put myself alongside many others, the poets, photographers, naturalists for whom walking has meant much more than simply traversing space.

The Ritual

I have decided on a walk that will be circular, to include four stages within a quite small area. Being a historian has taught me that often it is necessary to focus on the immediate if one is to address the larger questions, for the seemingly local and parochial can face us with what is fundamental, universal. I think of it as an aperture through which, from this small opening, I am addressing something great. I have decided that the stages of this walk will be marked by reference to the four elements. I have chosen them because, since time immemorial, when men and women have tried to make sense of the universe they have turned to these four foundational aspects of the known world: earth, air, water, fire – all of which must play their part in human experience. There is something ageless and elemental in the image of sowing and reaping: the seed lying in the earth in darkness, the rain which it needs as it emerges into the air, drawn by the light and warmth of the sun. Each one of the elements here has in turn its essential role to play. There are many different interpretations; they might be put in the form of a circle with fire placed on the outside and earth at the centre, and in between come water and air binding them together. Then they become magical in the hands of the Swiss alchemist Paracelsus who was the first to associate the earth with gnomes, the air with sylphs, water with undines and fire with salamanders![30] The Celtic imagination found seven elements, dividing the air into calm and tempest, and water into clear and salt, and finally adding flowers. I find this attractive, but I remain content with the traditional four.

I cannot walk in the area around the cottage without being aware of the pervasive presence of trees, and so I want to include wood on this walk. How many people have written in praise of trees! How many painters have struggled, like Paul Nash, to render 'the peculiar degree of beauty, of mystery', that they found in the features of trees.[31] Edward Thomas said that he liked trees 'for their cloudy forms linked to the earth by stately stems ... for their straight pillars and for the twisted branch work ... for their still shade and their rippling or calm shimmering or dimly glowing light ... for their solemnity and their dancing, for all their sounds and motions ... for their kindliness and their serene remoteness and inhumanity.'[32] These are the words of a poet and they make me look anew at the old oak which stands in the field opposite the gate, guardian of my coming and going. He listed oaks with sycamores, elms and beeches as the massiest of trees that have also 'the glory of motion'. And then there are the words attributed to John Chrysostom, well called the golden-voiced:

The tree is my eternal salvation.
It is my nourishment and my banquet.
Amidst its roots, I cast my own roots deep.
Beneath its bough I grow.
I flower with its fruits.
Its fruits bring perfect joy.
If I stumble this is my staff.
This is Jacob's ladder, where angels go up and down,
And where the Lord himself stands at the top.

I shall be touching bark as I walk, for I will be using my senses (but I shall be leaving out taste, something that always proves most challenging on any country walk except at the height of summer or early autumn). Sight and sound, touch and smell: all these senses will mean that I will walk slowly and deliberately, consciously aware of my surroundings. As so often, a traditional Celtic blessing comes to mind, and this is one that I frequently use since it reminds me of the interconnectedness between the human being and the earth. As I put my foot to the ground it is something reciprocal: I am both receiving blessing and giving blessing:

Bless to me, O God,
   The earth beneath my foot.
Bless to me, O God,
   The path where on I go.[33]

I begin by walking slowly up a winding lane towards the church, as I have done many hundreds of times before. The careless abundance of wildflowers that were here fifty years ago are gone now and I feel a nostalgia for what we have lost. Beyond the hawthorn hedgerows that have grown old and straggly, with spiky branches writhing and twisting, lie the fields whose names I know so well from old maps: they are a mixture of Welsh and Old English, describing the topography of the land – a big field, a narrow strip of land, birch trees. I repeat the words and get pleasure from the knowledge of their age, *Landesweane*, *Cae Maw*, *Wigga*. This is a peopled landscape, peopled by the living and the dead; here generation has succeeded generation on the land.

At the next bend a squat Norman church comes into view, and, glinting as it swings in the sun, is a golden cockerel on top of the sturdy tower. I go up a few stone steps into the churchyard and make for my destination, a bench beneath a vast, ancient yew. I love this spot; the age of this tree is reassuring, as is its tenacity and resilience. Even when it seems hollow and dying, new shoots will burst forth. It gives it an untidy, unruly appearance, gnarled and knotted, with roots stretching far and snaking up through the grass. It is sobering, although also curiously exhilarating, to reflect that this is probably the oldest living organism that I am ever likely to see.

From here I idly watch the swinging cockerel, that volatile reminder of the inconstancy of St Peter, his denial of Christ. Turning in the wind, this bird swings, stoutly facing in one direction after another, a signal of the weather as well as a reminder of the disciple.[34] With these two divergent images – the solidity of the tower and the versatility of the golden bird – playing in my mind, I look across the churchyard with its rows of stone tombstones, many of whose family names I know so well, and think of the certainty of mortality and the uncertainty that surrounds its timing. I love the decoration of the headstones: sometimes for a husband and wife, two clasped hands that speak of togetherness in this life and the next. Sometimes there are chubby cherubs with neatly folded wings, often looking half asleep and not on guard as they should rightly be.

No urns here, nothing pretentious. This is a rustic world in death as in life. I shall be buried here, in my chosen spot, under the yew, next to my sister and a most beloved grandson.

This is my first station, and here, as well as the wood of my sheltering tree, I encounter the first of my elements, earth, and reflect that it is Janus-faced – as they all are – affirmative and destructive, life-affirming and life-denying. The earth itself is essential to our life, our well-being, and yet an avalanche, a landslide, can crush and kill. I need air to breathe, but a tornado, a hurricane, tears all in its path. Without water life ceases, but floods overwhelm and drown. Fire is essential and necessary, yet there are few more destructive forces than a forest fire or an erupting volcano. So while I follow St Francis in praising the elements, I keep in mind that all is not simply beautiful. Nevertheless, *Laudato Si'* seems the appropriate hymn to recall as I sit under this ancient yew which could well date to the time of St Francis – who wrote this canticle in 1235. After he had celebrated the sun, moon and stars, his great paean moves on to the praise of the mystery and the sanctity of the elements, and God incarnate in the world around him.

> Praise be you, O my Lord, for our Brother Wind,
>   and for air and clouds, calm and all weather
>   through which you uphold life in all creatures.
> Praise the Lord for our Sister Water,
>   who is useful to us and humble and precious
>   and clean.
> Praise the Lord for our Brother Fire,
>   through whom you give us light in the darkness.
>   He is bright and pleasant and very mighty and strong.
> Praise the Lord for our Mother Earth,

who sustains and keeps us, and brings forth the grass
and all of the fruits and flowers of many colours.[35]

Sitting looking at the graves in front of me I think of those
words in the funeral service, 'dust thou art and to dust thou
shalt return': thou shalt return to the earth. At the graveside mourners are invited to let fall a handful of earth on to
the coffin below. It scatters as it hits the wood and rattles
with an echoing sound. In his long and moving poem,
which is simply entitled 'Earth', the priest-poet Malcolm
Guite shows us the bereaved clutching in his frozen hand
the handful of soil that he is about to throw:

Here at the graveside, holding onto earth.
The time approaches when he will let go.
But now his freezing fist is clenched as hard
As ice around the dirt of which we're made
And his poor heart is ice beneath the floe
Waiting for the moment of release.

The priest has told him that he should release
The earth he holds when he hears earth to earth
And dust to dust.[36]

I walk across the churchyard and go up to the church built
of the local red sandstone and stand for a moment with
my hand against the wall, like William Fiennes' father
drawing strength from the building. It is easy to love this
stone; I think of it as a steadfast presence in my life. I
find a comfortable place to sit on the churchyard wall
because before I leave I want to spend a little time thinking
about how this stone was quarried, dug from the ground
around here, shaped into the building blocks that went
to make this small twelfth-century Romanesque church.

I am helped to picture this by how it is described in one of my favourite novels, *The Stones of the Abbey*.[37] It is an account of the building of Le Thoronet, in which the stone itself plays a central role. 'I am defending more than just a material, I am defending my faith in matter itself.' Asked by the master-builder if he loves this local stone which is so difficult to handle, one of the monks replies: 'Yes, and I believe that the feeling is reciprocated. Since the very first day, I have had respect for it ... Now it is a part of myself ... I caress it in my dreams ... the sun sets on it, the rain darkens it and makes it glisten.' Every morning he visits the quarry, confronting this stone, refusing to use mortar or daub it with lime. 'I want to leave it a little freedom still, or it will not live.'

I reluctantly leave the wall and make my way up a small hill where the horizon opens out before me and I can see the line of Offa's Dyke in the distance, to a field that had once been a cider orchard and now has no more than two or three stunted moss-covered trees. I find a comfortable place in which to sit for my next station, grateful that I can lean my back against the trunk of one of these old apple trees, enjoying the texture of the rough bark. I gaze at huge cumulus clouds massing up, and watch them as they move and change with incessant play of shape and pattern. I have come here to think about my second element, the air. As if on cue two buzzards appear, making their familiar mewing sound, soaring effortlessly on leisurely wings higher and higher as they catch the air currents. There is amazing grace in their movement. I think of how they use the air, climbing to a great height, able to see vast distances and yet also able to drop like a plummet if they notice the slightest movement in the grass below. They give me a model: to have the widest horizons, yet to see the minute particulars. That is like this landscape, which has given me the sweeping views and breathtaking cloudscapes, and the secrecy of the hiddenness of tiny wild flowers folded into the grass. I stay still, thinking about the mystery of air and watching the clouds appear and disappear in an entrancing display. A butterfly approaches and I recognize it as a peacock. It flutters away and I leave this hill slope, saluting this sweeping view as I do so and bidding farewell to what has been so much a part of my interior landscape.

I walk down the slope of the hill to the river which flows below. I find a fallen tree, once a majestic oak, covered with moss, lying beside the river bank. It makes the perfect seat for my third station, in which I shall be thinking about the element of water. I settle down to watch the flowing stream. I am always drawn to running water. As I look at those swirling eddies, churning because the night before we had had rain, I reflect, as I have done so many times over the past fifty years, on the mystery of water, how its mood changes, how it is never the same, how its sounds differ and its colours vary. Sometimes it is so clear that I can count the pebbles in the shallows as they glint in the sun; then it will become dark as it drags up mud and scraps of wood, carrying them downstream with a fierce urgency. What had seemed gentle suddenly becomes turbulent and destructive – just like a buzzard in flight. To live beside water does not allow any easy and romantic approach to nature. It does, however, confront me with the mystery of time, that fluent moment in which the arrival and the leaving become one. Just sitting here and watching, almost mesmerized by the flow of the water I feel myself part of a wider world. I know so well how two small brooks have flowed together to make this larger stream, and I know where it will join the river Monnow and so flow on into the Wye. I know where the Wye rises in the uplands of Wales and where it will lose itself in the sea.

All this brings me back to the mystery of interconnectedness. I am only a small part of the whole. A confluence of
waters always carries significance, as my poet neighbour
Anne Cluysenaar wrote about this stream:

    a flow out of darkness,
    winding on each other
    like voices singing.
    ...
    These are its music,
    it's almost human
    chanting, its almost
    human leap
    into thin air.[38]

I turn and leave and start to make my way home, with a
couple of phrases from the psalms ringing in my mind:
'They shall drink from the river of your delight ... with
you is the well of life.' It is early dusk when I reach the
cottage. I go into the sitting room and light the fire that
I had already laid – taking pleasure in knowing where
all the wood has come from, whether small twigs for the
kindling or the great logs of wild cherry which hold the
structure in place on either side of the fireplace. I strike a
match and the flame is a tiny centre of light that I have to
cup in my hands to keep from dying. Then I coax it into
further flame and watch it creeping, getting stronger and
higher. There is something in this fire that speaks to me
tonight of my own life, and I am delighted that it is now
so strong. I have come here to my own hearth to think of
the final of four elements, the element of fire. Just like each
of the others it is both foundational and Janus-faced, for
it speaks both of what is domestic and what is destructive.
I take down from the corner of the mantelshelf the figure

of a Madonna and child and hold it in my hand, feeling its light solidity. It is made of volcanic ash. It comes from the Philippines, and I was given it on a visit to a community of Benedictine sisters. They had shown me a scene of devastation after a disastrous volcano, with a church half buried in ash. Yet here was something of simple beauty which quite literally came from dust and ashes. As I continue to hold it in my hand I feel a great sense of gratitude for those unknown hands that could fashion this, and show me that the new can be born from the old. Then as I watch the fire flicker and reflect on the symbolism of flame, there is nothing better than that well-known story from the Desert Fathers:

> Abbot Lot went to see Abbot Joseph and said to him, 'Abba, as far as I can I say my little office, I fast a little, I pray and meditate, I live in peace and as far as I can, I purify my thoughts. What else can I do?' Then the old man stood up and stretched his hands towards heaven. His fingers became like ten lamps of fire and he said to him, 'If you will, you can become all flame.'

Perhaps this is all that I want to say about fire. There are too many words – words of poetry and of prose, and I would rather leave it to words of prophecy and promise.

Letting Go – of Possessions

And now it is time to go. I walk from the sitting room, leaving the fire smouldering in the hearth and the smell of wood smoke, and I walk into the kitchen. The scrubbed wooden table stands there, the heart of the house. There are so many memories, of family celebrations, of visiting friends, of food and talk and happiness. There was always a lighted candle in the centre of the table, and after any gathering the youngest child present (provided that they were over three) was allowed to hold the long snuffer and put out the flame – and then we would sit and watch the curling smoke gently weaving patterns in the air as it changed colour. That was the little domestic ritual that marked the end of the meal. But now I need a ritual on a far larger scale, one that is for myself, one that is urgent to perform before I leave. I have never forgotten Donald

Nicholl, that wise teacher,[39] who had once said to me: 'Go round the house, touch each thing in turn and say, "Not mine – only on loan, not mine – only on loan".' This is now the task that I set myself. I make a start by placing my hand on the table and with gratitude saying my mantra out loud. Then I move towards the great old oak chest, once overflowing with children's toys; and so I go from room to room, sometimes pausing longer if there is a particular association, as with a beautiful bureau that had belonged to my mother. When I come to the bookcases many of the shelves are already half empty, for there has been a slow dismantling over the past few weeks, and great numbers of boxes have been sent off to Oxfam. This taking apart of a library built up over so many years is particularly painful, for here are books that have come to feel almost like an extension of my own personality, books reflecting my growing and changing interests over many years – architecture, botany, travel, poetry. Here the process of letting go becomes extraordinarily difficult, for, as Ben Okri says:

> To open a book is to open a world … between covers, genies reside in words. A book is an object that contains thousands of other objects – streets, houses, people, palaces, canals, dreams, skies, rivers, paintings, works of art, civilizations, centuries, stories, memories, futures, deaths, births, galaxies, histories, ideas. A book is a work of magic that never stops creating its magic.[40]

I stretch out my hand for one particular book and find it no longer there; there is a sudden stab, it feels like the loss of an old and cherished friend. I tell myself that I was allowed to enjoy its companionship but that there comes the time to pass it on. It brings home to me just how demanding is an attitude of non-possession. But I know that without it nothing new can grow. I think about Bruce Chatwin towards the very end of his life, in May 1988, living at Ipsden near Oxford, making plans for what he wants to do, but 'I cannot do this work if I am fettered to possessions. I have envied and grasped at possessions but they are very bad for me. I want to be free of them.'[41]

We do not own the world or any part of it; 'we hold it in an everlasting lease'. How often in the past have I used those wonderful words of Thomas Traherne to talk on this theme of seeing the world as a place of gifts not a place of objects to be acquired or consumed. Now I have to live it out. And so, as so often, I turn to the sixth-century Rule of St Benedict for practical guidance. It has played a vital role in my life ever since the Canterbury days when I first encountered St Benedict. It was purely fortuitous (or possibly God's celestial time-keeping?). We were living in the tied cottage that goes with the job of Dean of Canterbury, a house that was the prior's lodging in the Middle Ages when Canterbury had been one of the greatest of medieval monastic communities. I loved the thought of our family life with four sons growing up in a place with a monastic past, and, wanting to discover more, I picked up this sixth-century Rule, looking on it as no more than a piece of historical evidence. Instead I found a way of life to which I could immediately relate. Written for a community, it had much wisdom for relationships in family life. But above all it made sense for a lay person, for the Prologue, a lyrical piece of writing, addresses the individual with an urgency that is quite compelling. I thought of the irony of having grown up in a Shropshire vicarage where my father was the vicar of a parish church which had once been a Benedictine priory, and how that had meant nothing to me except lists of dates of land charters and the names of priors. Now the Benedictine way of life became one that I tried to follow, and so, faced with questions about ownership and possessions, it was natural to turn to St Benedict for guidance. And indeed I found the help that I was seeking.

In a memorable aphorism, St Benedict told his monks that they were to treat the goods and chattels of the monastery as though they were the sacred vessels of the altar. Everything matters. Material things are to be handled with reverence and respect, but at the same time with detachment, since in a community where all things are held in common nothing might be claimed as personal property. We see the implications of this in a chapter on work, for important truths are often presented in practical situations.[42] The tools of the monastery are to be handed out to the brothers, and the abbot keeps a list because these things are on loan, to be handled with care until the due time of return. The Latin word that is used here is *recolligenda*, the same word that is used for harvesting, so the connotation is that of a crop coming to the time of fulfilment. Then the question will be: did things flourish in my hands? This is good stewardship. St Benedict recognizes the dangers of possessiveness as a deep fault line running through our lives. I tell myself time and again of the dangers of wanting to possess. Everything is gift. Pope Francis, in *Let us Dream*, does not hesitate to call possessiveness a sin. He says that our sin lies in failing to recognize value, in wanting to possess and exploit that which we do not value as gift. And then he puts it starkly: sin always has this same root of possessiveness. I ask myself if this is a time when I should make a list of the possessions which have hitherto enriched me, and make a conscious act of thanksgiving for the part that they have played in my life and the value that they have brought – and then let them go.

Letting Go – of People

But then I have to face the letting go of the people in my life and what that asks of me. I think back with gratitude to our marriage, our family life and not least the places associated with that. I got married at Cambridge, although not as an undergraduate. I was a research fellow at Newnham College and Victor the Succentor of King's College. Two sons were born in Cambridge and two at Nottingham where Victor had become the university chaplain. Good years were followed by even better when we moved to Lincoln, when Victor was appointed as Chancellor of the cathedral. That appointment carried with it a house, the Chancery, with which we all immediately fell in love. It was huge and old and rambling, with room for everyone to explore enthusiasms and make collections and organize museums. Everyone blossomed there in a place that encouraged creativity. When suddenly Victor accepted the post of Dean of Canterbury I was devastated. It felt like an uprooting from all that had become loved and significant in my life – a city set on a hill with its most beautiful cathedral, the friends living around us in Minster Yard, the students of the theological college. We had been there for seven years, and I so organized it that the moving vans would come on the same date in August as that of our arrival – it was a symbolic statement about our seven good years there. But I also devised my own secret ritual, by walking the length of the south side of the cathedral on the evening when the bellringers held their practice. Against that evocative sound I repeated to myself a phrase that I had found in the writings of E. F. Benson (made the more meaningful because he had grown up in the Chancery exactly a century before when his father Edward White Benson had been Chancellor). 'The world-wonder of beauty' became like a mantra, expressing my sense of loss of this amazing place.

And now the Canterbury years unfolded. The four sons grew up and successively left home, in the first instance to do adventurous things before they went up to university – India, Tanzania, Japan, Russia. I was immensely proud of their initiative. As I said goodbye to each in turn, I took note of the date so that I would be able to recall it later. It is not always easy to let go of one's children. Yet the art of loving a person is letting them go free. It is expressed simply by C. Day-Lewis in his poem 'Walking Away':

Selfhood begins with a walking away
And love is proved in the letting go.[43]

I was at the time exploring the Celtic tradition and finding that the poems and blessings that had come down through the generations in the Hebrides often expressed feelings very simply and immediately. There is one prayer which asks for the blessing on a son or daughter as they leave home, perhaps for a future far away. I love the physicality with which it opens:

Be the great God between thy two shoulders
To protect thee in thy going and in thy coming.
Be the Son of Mary Virgin near thy heart
And the perfect Spirit upon thee pouring –
Oh, the perfect Spirit upon thee pouring.[44]

The letting go of a spouse is infinitely more painful. Canterbury came to an end after ten years, but it was an abrupt ending, which allowed for no farewells or leave-taking. That beautiful house had to be taken apart, and anything that was of any size had to be got rid of, since the cottage was now to be our permanent home and that was small and already furnished. Anything that had served us so happily for entertaining vast numbers of people now had no future. The elegant Victorian sewing table was sent for sale, as was the musical box, both of which had belonged to the grandmother whom I had never known but for whom I had been named – the ending of one of my few links with her. So many of the things that had to go carried memories. I remember standing in the hall looking up at Bell Harry and telling myself that we were only a small part of the story of this place and would soon be forgotten. It did little to lift my mood. Equally painful was leaving the cathedral itself. I had come to know it so well, and with real knowledge came real love. I went into it for the last time to visit the two places that meant the most to me. I entered by the crypt door, felt the strength of its Romanesque pillars and its warm enclosing darkness. Then I climbed the steps to the Corona Chapel at the furthest eastern point of the cathedral, flooded with light. It was dominated by the glorious Redemption window, which takes the story of Christ's life from death to resurrection, from ascension to Pentecost. The cathedral was deserted. I sang the doxology under my breath, and left.

After this we were there together at the cottage for a number of years. I had begun to give retreats and to lecture and travel: Victor spent six months in Zimbabwe. We were both involved with a convent and also with a retreat house in Wales. It was here that Victor decided that he would be happier living. When he made the decision to leave I asked him if it could be on some meaningful day so that I could recall it later. So it was on 6 August, the feast of the Transfiguration, that he went. The date was also that of the dropping of the bomb on Hiroshima, a place that we had once visited together, and so the day carried an image both of the light and the dark, a suitable paradox for the ending of a relationship. Before we parted we had a very simple ceremony in a nearby church, Llangua, lying in a field in a bend of the River Wye. At the end of Evensong we asked for a blessing from the priest, an old friend, and I gave back my wedding ring. Then we had the hymn that we had had at our wedding, the words of Charles Wesley, 'O thou who camest from above'. So with this ritual we separated. There was still, however, one thing that bound us, the prayer of Henry VI, dating from those early years in Cambridge and our connection with King's College.

Domine Jesu Christe,
qui me creasti,
redemisti et preordinasti
ad hoc quod sum,
tu scis quid de me facere vis;

fac de me secundum
voluntatem tuam
cum misericordia.
Amen.

O Lord Jesus Christ
Who hast created
and redeemed me,
and hast brought me
to that which I now am,
thou knowest what thou wouldst do with me
do with me according to thy will
for thy tender mercy's sake.
Amen.

It had been easy in the past, when taking retreats or giving lectures, to talk romantically about solitude, the solitary life, the hermit existence. I had been fond of quoting early Celtic lyrics which spoke of how idyllic it was, or the Trappist Thomas Merton speaking of the delight of his hermitage in the woods in Kentucky. I loved in particular those verses which took the form of a conversation between two brothers, one living at court, the other as a hermit:

I have a hut in a wood: only my Lord knows it; an ash closes it on one side, and a hazel like a great tree on the other.
The size of my hut small, not too small, a homestead with familiar paths ...
Beautiful are the pines which make music for me unhindered: through Christ I am no worse off than you.[45]

But the solitary life was not always as idyllic as the hermit made out. It was lonely. It felt sad to cook only for oneself.

I missed the easy companionship in the evenings, sitting beside the fire, reading or in casual conversation about the day's happenings. There was no one to rescue me when a bat got into my bedroom. At the garage I struggled to put air into the tyres. There was no one there to welcome me when I returned from travelling, no one to tell about what I had been doing, to share the failures or the successes, to help me to debrief. But worst of all the depression, which has always haunted my life, once more circled around me. I still continued to write and to prepare material for engagements. I had deadlines to meet, commitments to honour, and that helped me to get on with daily living even when it seemed a heavy burden. I turned to Thomas Merton, a man so complex that whatever mood I was in I could find echoes in his experience. I was writing a book about him, for which his monastery, Gethsemani, had generously given me some of his photographs with which to illustrate it. These I propped up on the kitchen table where I could see them when I was at work. They were simply the ordinary utensils of his daily life in his hermitage – a log basket, a workman's glove thrown on to a stool, a battered jug – or of natural objects in the immediate surroundings of the woods – an old tree stump, tangled roots. There was a contemplative quality about them which had a calming, restoring effect. They also carried with them an immediacy that helped me to live in the present moment. He was telling me through the way in which he handled the camera a truth I already knew deep down but needed to repeat to myself time and again – life must be lived in the present moment. The past is past, I must let it go; the future is unknown, the only reality lies in the present.

'Every important creative act has this duality: of giving everything and then letting go, so that the created thing can have a life of its own.' The voice of an artist speaks of what she knows from her own experience.[46] Celia Paul is a painter, but the art of letting go touches something that is deep in us all. Loving and letting go is at the heart of God's love for the world: ours is a God who loves us so much that he lets us go into a freedom which allows us to either accept or reject that love. Letting go or self-emptying is clearly the way of Jesus: his own life, death and resurrection show us how to gain by losing.

Simplicity

I have been given the chance to have a life of greater simplicity. 'Give me simplicity, that I may live,' says George Herbert in his poem 'A Wreath', which John Drury calls his 'singing prayer'. Herbert articulates for me, as any good poet always does, just what I want to say:

> So live and like, that I may know thy ways
> Know them and practice them.[47]

The minimalist architect John Pawson tells us that it was the oppressive weight of possessions that gave him his first taste for simplicity. He believes that restraint has produced some of the most beautiful work that the world has ever seen. He explores this in a small book, *Minimum*,[48] looking at its expression over many centuries and many cultures.

Among far-ranging subjects it is particularly his discussion of the Shakers and of the Cistercians that brought me the greatest enjoyment. I have visited one or two Shaker settlements in America, and it is significant that the title Thomas Merton gave to the book he wrote about them should be *Religion in Wood*. Shakers with their communal way of life and freedom from the encumbrance of personal possessions produced both buildings and artefacts of remarkable intensity, beauty and perfection. It was said of their furniture that each chair was made so that it was fit for an angel to sit on. Their houses are restful, their staircases elegant. It was not so much their skill (for they would exchange jobs) as their determination to eliminate the inessential that gave to whatever they handled what John Pawson has called a transcendent quality.

One of his favourite places, and one from which he drew inspiration, was the twelfth-century Cistercian abbey of Le Thoronet in Provence, which he had first visited at the insistence of the writer Bruce Chatwin and afterwards returned to each year. He found here a functional beauty which grew out of the ideals of St Bernard of Clairvaux seeking a humble simplicity in the lives of his monks. The Cistercian reform movement of the twelfth century sought to regain the original purity of the Rule of St Benedict, lost through a prosperity and worldliness that was reflected in rich and decorated buildings. In contrast, Cistercian architecture shows the monastic ideals of simplicity and self-denial. Hidden, away from the eyes of the world, the churches that they built in their period of greatest expansion (between 1130 and 1150) were buildings of sublime beauty. In their hands, poverty, restraint and austerity became sources of strength. The use of indigenous materials, and minimum decoration, brought a sense of harmony and purity. It can be seen at Le Thoronet where the unity between the natural and the man-made is profoundly restful: it is as though the abbey is rising seamlessly from the ground itself. Le Corbusier spoke of its truth, tranquillity and strength when he wrote the introduction to Lucien Hervé's photographic portrait, *The Architecture of Truth*, and John Pawson simply said: 'Le Thoronet remains for me the most beautiful building in the world.'[49]

Simplicity is the ideal that will sustain me while I am deep in the task of decluttering. There can be few things more mundane than tossing one's material possessions into an already overflowing skip. Sometimes it can feel like an amputation, but that is rather overdramatic: it is only what thousands of other people have done. Bonnie Thurston writes of her experience of her parents' packing up:

We are decisively cut adrift
from the past's moorings,
forced to look ahead instead of back.
Like Abram to gain the promise,
we leave country, kindred, father's house.
Now we make our own home place.
Now we must be present where we are.[50]

Lament

But before I can be 'present where I am' there is the time of cutting adrift, of leaving the home place. The Welsh have the word *hiraeth*, which is not easily translated but means a deep longing for home, and carries a sense of anguish, of longing sorrow, a yearning for home and for one's homeland. Homesickness is a very real affliction, and in the past recognized as such and named as a medical condition, with definite symptoms. James Copland, drawing on earlier writers, in his *Dictionary of Practical Medicine* published in 1858, said of homesickness that it was 'amongst the most distressing of the numerous ills that embitter the destiny of men'.[51] He found numerous examples of the continued longing for the scenes of early life; of patients characterized by unusual reserve and sadness; and of decline, pallor and painful rumination.

Copland continues: 'the patient nurses his misery, augments it until it destroys his nightly repose and his daily peace, and ultimately devours, with more or less rapidity, his vital organs'. He then concludes that such nostalgia required more of a moral than a medical intervention. The original meaning of the word nostalgia is well revealed by Renée Hirschon who points out its Greek roots, *nostos* (returning home), *algos* (ache, pain, homesickness). She makes a valuable contrast with current English usage, quoting *The New Oxford Dictionary of English*, which gives us a rather trivializing and superficial definition – 'wistful affection' or 'sentimental longing'. Instead it is a word which reflects the deep emotional bonds associated with place and the disruption and suffering experienced when separated from the place.[52] She writes of forced displacement and although I cannot place myself in that category, nevertheless what she says strikes chords with my own situation and allows me to take it seriously, for, she says, it entails the disruption of the self, of the matrix of identity, of the social fabric to which one belongs, and thus of the whole person. Again I am brought back to the extent to which the sense of person and the sense of place are indissolubly bound together in most societies.

Leaving feels like an uprooting. The Welsh have a fierce sense of belonging. *O le dach chi'n yr wreiddiol?* – where do you come from originally? Or, more literally, where do you come from *in your roots*? I have an image of the struggle needed to uproot some tenacious plant or some young sapling, and this helps me not to feel too guilty that my own uprooting should cause me pain. And that pain has to be owned. I accept it, knowing that healing comes with time. Now I am going to give myself permission to have a time of lamentation. Without this I cannot truly be myself. Henri Nouwen, who knew much about suffering, asks the pertinent question: am I taking my wounds to my head or to my heart? To try to deal with them in a purely cerebral way will not be helpful. When Gerard Manley Hopkins lamented the cutting down of a line of poplars in Binsey, the words he wrote read like a cry of pain:

> My aspens dear, whose airy cages quelled,
> Quelled or quenched in leaves the leaping sun,
> All felled, felled, are all felled ...[53]

Lament has been a feature of the human race since time immemorial, often a public outpouring by which a people could express their shared loss. The book of Lamentations is the desperate expression of a people's grief and despair at the destruction of the Temple at Jerusalem in 587 BC. It is so vivid: 'My eyes are spent with weeping ...' And yet, right in the middle of this very short book of only five chapters, comes a huge affirmation of the mercy of a God whose steadfast love never ceases. 'The Lord is my portion, therefore will I hope in him', and then, 'The Lord is good unto them that wait for him.' That is sorrow which is public and shared. But there are also individual voices giving play to grief: David crying out at the death of a beloved son, Rachel weeping for her children. Above all there are the tears of Christ, after the death of Lazarus. The scene is so vividly told in St John's Gospel (John 11.20–35) where first Martha and then Mary reproach him for arriving too late to save their brother. But his tears are not for Lazarus whom, after all, he will soon raise from the dead. They are, says Erik Varden, the abbot of the Cistercian abbey of Mount St Bernard, tears for the sight of humanity weeping. They have much in common with Virgil's *lacrimae rerum*, the tears of things, the acknowledgement that this world, in its brittle beauty, is broken.[54]

Today we have lost the habit and the tradition but not the need for lamentation. Peter Levi, the former Jesuit, gave his inaugural lecture as Professor of Poetry in the University of Oxford on the subject of lamentation of the dead.[55] He paid special attention towards the end of his lecture to a landscape that he knew well, that of Greece and in particular the Mani. These traditional outpourings touch me because they have the same style and simplicity as those dirges orally collected in the Outer Hebrides at virtually the same time, in the late nineteenth century. They are the voices of country people who need to situate their grief in the land that they know.

> I shall arise at break of dawn, the sun two hours unrisen,
> I will take water, I will wash, water and I will waken,
> and I will take the track, the track, the path so beautiful
> ...

This encourages me to let the pain of loss find expression, just as did all those nameless voices of the past who knew that to speak their own words of loss was something natural and healing. So in my imagination I picture an autumn day at the cottage, autumn being my favourite season of the year. I like to follow the Celtic calendar in which autumn starts in August, with the feast of Lammas, the gathering in of the fruits on 1 August, and it ends on 1 November, with the feast of Samhaine, which marks the start of winter. So I write my own lament for a place and a season:

Elegy for Autumn

Gone is the sound of the river at the waterfall.
Gone is the night sky and the stars high above my head.
Gone is the moon whose waxing and waning has
  accompanied my path.
Gone are the owls at nightfall echoing one another
  down the valley.
Gone are the wild berries in the hedges that I know
  so well.
Gone are the apples to be gathered and stored with
  loving attention.
Gone are the leaves changing colour and falling, each
  according to their nature.
Gone are the bonfires with their careful, loving, lighting
  ... with their brilliant flames and their coils of smoke.
Gone is the Harvest Festival when young and old
  congregate year by year to celebrate the blessings of
  the earth.

When John Clare said adieu to the trees and the plants that he loved so well on leaving Helpston, he felt that this loss was mutual: the favourite spots that have known him for so long 'seem bidding me farewell'.[56] Will the waterfall, the owls, the trees miss my presence? The seasons will turn and new life will begin. Grief will diminish with time, although it may not fully disappear. I write words addressed in the first instance to myself, because they help me to deal with the ache of longing that is homesickness. Times of darkness are bound to return. Christian Bobin was a lifelong sufferer from persuasive melancholy and spent most of his life 'mining the narrow seam of joy in the dank rock face of depression'. Writing was the tool he employed to chip it out. He uses the imaginative images

of a poet: 'Whenever anguish shows up I put it in a suitcase and slide it under my bed. From time to time I pull
the suitcase out and open it. There is nothing in it, or a
luminous little fruit tree.'[57]

I am glad of this reminder. Sorrow is acceptable, self-
pity is not. Thankfulness ought to be easy but it isn't. That
is why I am grateful when W. H. Auden speaks of the
need to practise the scales of rejoicing, because it reminds
me of the sort of discipline that I should be looking for in
myself. Gratefulness and letting go come together as the
next chapter of my life starts.

Arrival

I cross the threshold. I have been here before of course with measuring tape in hand, planning for this moment. And now it has come and I am taking my first step into my new life. At first, inevitably, it is a scene of organized confusion. But then it is done and I look around me. I greet my furniture, a few pictures, my remaining books, and enjoy the new relationships that they now make as I arrange my sitting room and my bedroom. I greet familiar things and ask for their companionship in a new situation; I want to welcome them, and hope that they will soon give the appearance of belonging here. I want this above all to be a place where I shall feel at home, a place that welcomes me as I step through the door, and a place where I can welcome friends, a place of hospitality.

Just as I had a ritual for saying farewell, now I need one

for arriving. To embrace the new asks for courage and flexibility; I want to make a start by seeking a blessing on the place where I shall most probably live for the rest of my life. There is a tradition of chalking on the doorpost the letters C+M+B at the time of arrival, so I make a start by putting Christus Mansionem Benedicat, Christ bless this house. I next turn to the *Carmina Gadelica*, because here are the prayers and praises of a people who knew so much about the interconnectedness of the material and spiritual as they experienced it in the home and in the hallowing of daily life. I find a very simple blessing:

> Be Christ's cross on your new dwelling,
> Be Christ's cross on your new hearth,
> Be Christ's cross on your new abode,
> Upon your new hearth blazing.[58]

As I look around me a phrase from a favourite psalm comes to mind: 'the lot marked out for me is my delight' (Psalm 15). Settling in will take time, and I should expect it to be a slow process. Here is something new and I want to foster its growth gently and with respect. Instead of a house, an annexe and a garden I now have two rooms, an apartment, on the second floor of a large building. It is in a wonderful location. It is true that no longer do I open my door on to a garden – a long corridor is not the same thing. Nevertheless, I am here. I am alone. The removal men have driven back to Herefordshire, the helping son has returned to London. Before I go to bed I sit on a chair by the window – I silently apologize to it that it is no longer in its accustomed place. When I open the window there are new sounds: traffic on a busy road instead of the sound of water, some trees but not yet my trees, and very distantly the chimes of Great Tom from Christ Church. I must learn to enjoy the sound of traffic and these new trees. There is work to be done in re-rooting and it must begin here and now on this summer evening. I find resonances with May Sarton in her poem 'Now I become myself':

Now to stand still, to be here,
Feel my own weight and density! ...
Now there is time and Time is young.
O, in this single hour I live
All of myself and do not move.[59]

Now is the time to still the running of my mind. I am so tempted to look back or to plan ahead, but for this evening I need stillness, simply knowing that I am alive, savouring the present moment, silently holding it before God. The past is behind me now, the future has yet to unfold. How much has been written about the importance of living in the present moment. How many daily reminders there are. St Benedict is insistent that we live *cotidie*, today. The Lord's Prayer, said twice daily, situates us firmly in this day – daily bread, daily forgiveness. The Venite, sung daily, insists that we listen *today* for the voice of God. A new place and the possibilities of new beginnings; each day sufficient to itself, each moment to be lived as fully as possible. While I recognize how right this is, there is a part of me that takes delight in Sydney Smith's advice on living only from day to day: 'take short views of human life – never further than dinner or tea'.

Now my task is to make my new home ordered, calm. The books are in chaos. I am faced by old grocery boxes filled to overflowing. Familiar cooking utensils go into unfamiliar cupboards. My Staffordshire cows and sheep which looked well in a cottage kitchen seem out of place here. I struggle with it all. But it is only a question of time. Covid makes it the more urgent since now I shall be spending so much more time indoors. This is a time when literature and art can help. I was fascinated by something I read about those paintings of seventeenth-century Dutch interiors that I thought I knew so well. Those Dutch masters painted scenes of calm, ordered rooms and beautiful still lives at a time when the Low Countries were still in a state of war. For them the Motherland was not the state but the home to which one can return, an inhabitable, welcoming space. This is what I am now setting out to create – an ordered beauty in the context of a world in confusion.[60]

The Psalms

It is strange to be embarking upon a new life when one has reached old age. Yet in the psalms, which have long been my journeying songs, newness is a constant theme: 'I will give you a new heart and put a new spirit within you.' The psalms ring out the good news. Newness is a cause of rejoicing: in a process of continual transformation. God is bringing the new out of the old. St Augustine calls us singers of a new song. In a homily on St John's Gospel, he says: 'We become new men and new women, heirs of the new testament, singers of a new song.'[61] In Isaiah we read: 'Remember not the former things ... Behold I will do a new thing' (Isaiah 43.18–19). This message is an undercurrent of both the Old and the New Testaments. In Christ we become a new creation, the old order passes and all things are renewed. I should not dwell on the past for

God is about to do something new. But I must participate with divine activity. I take to heart the example of Lot's wife, told so succinctly in Genesis when she, leaving the city with her husband, 'looked back from behind him, and she became a pillar of salt'. She could not face the future, she longed for what she has left.

God is always at work, present, reaching out with covenant love. I can be sure of God's faithfulness. Psalm 40 expresses it so well in a new translation:

> I waited patiently for you, my God,
> and at last you heard my cry.
> You lifted me out of the icy torrent,
> you drew me out of the quicksand and mire.
>
> You set my feet on solid ground,
> making firm my foothold on rock.
> No longer am I empty and lost:
> you have given my life new meaning.
> You have put a new song in my mouth,
> a song of thanksgiving and praise.[62]

This is a time when the psalms mean more than ever before. If I turn to them for comfort and support, as also for rejoicing, I am only doing what countless people before me have done down the ages. St Ambrose describes them in euphoric terms. 'What is more pleasing than the psalm? In it teaching is combined with charm; for it is sung for pleasure but learnt for instruction.' He called the book of psalms delightful – 'Although the whole of sacred scripture breathes the spirit of God's grace, this is especially true of that delightful book, the book of the psalms.' He comments on their role compared with other Scripture: 'History instructs, the law disciplines, prophecy foretells, correction shows us our faults and morality suggests what should be done: but in the book of the psalms there is something more than all this and at the same time a sort of medicine for man's spiritual health.' He uses the image of the gymnasium, the stadium where different sorts of exercises are set out, the musical instrument of virtues. But above all it is the singing of praise; we should 'sing and praise the Lord in our hearts: My lips will shout for joy when I sing praises to you.'[63]

I sometimes read them in the familiar King James version that I have known since childhood, sometimes in new translations such as that of Jim Cotter, which bring fresh insights, jolting me into deeper understanding. In the psalter I find the songs of a journeying people: they accompany me through every stage and every mood of life. I can read, chant, sing, shout and above all pray them over and over again, and still they can surprise me by their freshness. The brevity of phrasing is one of the things that makes them so attractive. For, above all, the psalms use words economically and with restraint. When Jesus said, in his teaching on prayer in Matthew 6.7, 'Do not go on babbling like the heathen who imagine the more they say the more likely they are to be heard', I wonder if he had the psalms in mind? In his chapter on prayer, St Benedict also warns that prayer should be short and pure: 'We must know that God regards our purity of heart and tears of compunction, not our many words.'[64] Had he in mind Jesus' sayings on prayer?

Often the psalms bring me words that sing, which stay in my memory – it is very like holding a small stone in the palm of my hand (the white stone?), and weighing it, feeling delight. The Latin word for weight is *pondus,* so I ponder these words, as Mary did in her heart. Every day when I pray the psalms, phrases emerge simply and naturally, beautifully crafted. I will choose one and copy it, and place it where I can see it. It is a daily gift:

> For with you is the well of life
> and in your light shall we see light.

> You gave me freedom for my steps;
> my feet have never slipped.

> Make me hear rejoicing and gladness,
> that the bones you have crushed may revive.

> The Lord is my strength and my song.

> Watching and waiting.

My mood swings, but wherever I am I can find echoes in the psalms, for here is the whole range of human experience, from the deepest of despair to rapturous praise; every aspect of humanity spoken about, prayed about, reflected on. Many are suffused with a sense of the created world. They allow me to lament, to cry out in anguish and distress, in desolation to raise my fist at God; but they also effect a transformation into joy and rejoicing. I turn to them now, at a time when I want to articulate my feelings of sorrow and loss, even of exile, as well as a steadfast hope for the future. They hold together two voices: the voice of pain, anger and loss, and the voice of praise, certainty, confidence. They are wonderfully honest; they do not give me easy words or easy answers. There are psalms that cry out in sorrow, grief, lament; there are psalms that are full of joy, ringing out with praise and gratitude. 'You will make me hear joy and laughing.' These swings (which sometimes seem almost like sudden lurches) echo the swings in my own mood, the sudden changes that occur particularly at a time of uncertainty. But the psalms tell me that the darkness can be transformed into joy – and that it happens time and time again. It is an amazing message! So here I meet with joy and sorrow, expectation and fear, desperation and peace. The psalms can be tormented, turbulent, aggressive; they allow me to voice these negative feelings. But then, I am given the image of taking the Babylonian babies and dashing them against the rocks; the final verse of Psalm 137 (an image which troubled many people) tells me that I must take these negative thoughts while they are still nascent, before they are fully grown, and dash them against the rock that is Christ.[65] How often have I been grateful for that vivid picture!

Some psalms are intimate, others speak on behalf of a whole nation. Sometimes psalms will speak of fullness and riches, at other times of poverty and emptiness. All these different emotions play their part in my own life. When you take the psalms seriously you very quickly come into touch with some basic realities about human nature. For the Israelites in exile, when it seemed that their God had failed them, the only way to keep hope alive was to sing the poetry of the psalms. How poignant the cry in Psalm 137.1:

By the waters of Babylon,
there we sat down and there we wept.

In contrast how different the tone of the longest psalm in the book, Psalm 119, a celebration of the Torah, the Law, the Living Way, the living God in a loving covenant with his people. Those sections which sometimes seem to go on interminably repetitive are likened by Jim Cotter to facets of a diamond, each section a facet illuminating an aspect of the wisdom of God:

Teach me, O Lord, the way of thy statutes:
and I shall keep it unto the end. (v. 33)

My delight shall be in your statutes,
and I will not forget your word. (v. 16)

And I will walk at liberty
for I seek thy precepts. (v. 45)

Oh! How I love thy law.
It is my meditation all the day. (v. 97)

Thy word is a lamp unto my feet
and a light unto my path. (v. 105)

But above all, the psalms are songs of praise. When he
made his new translation from the Hebrew, the artist Roger
Wagner called the psalter *The Book of Praises*, since, as
he says in his Introduction, praise is the *cantus firmus*, the
fixed song, that sounds throughout them all. The whole
psalter is an edifice of praise, built on Psalm 1. The very
first word is blessed, then comes delight in the Torah, and
the image of being like a tree planted by streams of water,
bearing fruit in due season. And the psalter ends with
Psalm 150, just one huge outpouring of praise. Nothing is
too far or too near, and every conceivable musical instrument is brought into play:

We praise you in a glorious symphony.
We praise you on the lute and harp.
We praise you with the caress of the trumpet.
We praise you with the solace of the cello.[66]

This is the conclusion to the psalms of praise, and the end of the entire book of the psalms. Jim Cotter gives this as the concluding verse:

> Let everything that breathes under the sun,
> let the voices of our ancestors of old,
> let worlds unknown, within and beyond,
> all on this glad day give you praise.[67]

The great psalms of praise, said Thomas Merton, are the psalms par excellence, 'they are more truly Psalms than all the others, for the real purpose of a Psalm is to praise God'. He was writing, still comparatively early on in his years at Gethsemani, a small booklet *On the Psalms*, whose purpose was to encourage the layman (*sic*) to use the psalter. So he writes about praise:

> St Augustine says that God has taught us to praise Him, in the Psalms, not in order that He may get something out of this praise, but in order that we may be made better by it. Praising God in the words of the Psalms we can come to know Him better. Knowing Him better we love Him better, loving Him better we find our happiness in Him.[68]

When I pray the psalms I feel myself linked to those lamenting in Babylon, or to the early Christians under imperial persecution, to the Desert Fathers and Mothers, or to the medieval monasteries and convents – all of whom sang the psalms as the core of their daily worship. I can pray them as part of a monastic community or a parish congregation, but I can also pray them on my own, whether in the cottage or in my new home, knowing that many others will be using the selfsame words. So I think with gratitude of how today throughout the world nuns and monks will be meeting together for the *opus Dei*, the work of God. The knowledge of this brings me a sense of strength through this interconnectedness. Not for nothing are they sometimes called the canonical hours (the word canon originally meaning a measuring rod), since it is by its differing moods that a day is measured. But canon can also mean trellis, like a lattice that supports vines, so here is another image: the frame by which the daily monastic life is supported. 'Seven times a day will I praise you,' sings the psalmist – although the hours grow to eight with the addition of compline at nightfall, to make complete a day that may have begun before dawn So eight times a day, men and women living under monastic vows, together with lay members and guests, will assemble in choir to keep the appointed times in prayer and praise.

As Henri Nouwen became more at home with the life of the Trappist Abbey of the Genesee when he went there to live for seven months, he grew to love the psalms. He found that they began to weave themselves into his life.

How happy are those who no longer need books but carry the psalms in their hearts wherever they are or wherever they go. Maybe I should start learning the psalms by heart so that nobody can take them from me ... if I am ever subjected to hunger, pain, torture or humiliation ... the psalms will keep my spirit alive.[69]

There is a moving example of what this can mean – indeed it is the turning point – in the film *The Elephant Man*. The central figure is this hideously disfigured man, who seems scarcely human, who is apparently unable to speak and as a result has become a circus freak. Quite suddenly he is overheard reciting the twenty-third psalm, in the St James version, word for word, in perfect English. This must have been the secret nourishment of a lonely and suffering man. He must have carried those healing words in the silence of his heart for many years.

Silence is the key to Jim Cotter's book of his new translations of the psalms which carries the significant title *Out of the Silence . . . Into the Silence*. The times for pause and for silence that he includes are vitally important. Unlike monasteries where there is a background of silence, and where the community sitting in choir always pauses at the colon to bring a moment of silence, we have to punctuate the words of our praying with as much silence as we can. 'Start with silence, and let the words rise out of the depths of the silence and fall back into silence.' We should say a line out aloud, Jim Cotter tells us, and then imagine that we hear it back like an echo from the other side of the valley ... He gives us another analogy, that of lobbing a pebble into a still pool and watching the ripples move gently outwards until they reach the shore, and then lobbing in another pebble. In this way the psalms will enter into ourselves, become part of our being.

The Monastic Tradition

'If you hear his voice today, do not harden your hearts.'
St Benedict quotes from Psalm 95 in the Prologue to the
Rule, and that psalm, the Venite, was sung daily in the
monastery – as it is also sung by Anglicans using Cranmer's
Book of Common Prayer, since he took the monastic
offices and shortened them for lay usage. St Benedict's
love of the psalms is evident, not only that he quotes them
more frequently than any other book of the Bible but that
they are foundational in his daily pattern of the monastic
opus Dei. I come back again and again the older I get to
appreciate the role that the monastic tradition plays in my
life. There are so many monasteries where I feel at home,
where I am welcomed as a sister. I have never wanted to
become an oblate, which would tie me too directly to any
one of them; I do not want to label myself as belonging to
one particular place or one denomination, for each has its

own particular charism, and a different role to play in my life. My imagination takes me to a deeply pastoral part of Normandy and to Bec Hellouin, where the brothers and sisters live at either end of a valley – which St Anselm called 'mon petit nid', my little nest, when reluctantly he left it to become Archbishop of Canterbury. I have visited it so often that I can picture myself sitting in the sisters' chapel, then walking the road to the abbey, listening to the bell peal out from the ancient tower, and finally entering the abbey church as shards of light stream in and pour across the stone floor. Then I think of West Park, above the Hudson river in upstate New York. In my imagination I am standing outside the refectory with the first cup of coffee of the day in my hand, watching a spectacular sunrise. Here the brothers have made me a Companion and I sit in choir with them. I travel further in my mind in the USA and reach St John's Collegeville, with its most magnificent abbey church by Marcel Breuer, with its campus and its press and its great aesthetic achievement in the St John's Bible, reflecting the belief that the religious imagination has a role to play in bringing people to the gospel. Here as I wait in the abbey church I let that immense space enfold me and I think back to that Pentecost Sunday when I addressed the graduands and was in turn myself given an honorary degree, and that brings a very real sense of belonging. So I feel links to each of these three places, all following the Rule of St Benedict, all having the *opus Dei* in common, each with its distinctive God-given charism. Each has in turn brought a particular dimension to my understanding of the monastic life. In my mind I picture the church and hear the chant of each place, and know that I am a sister there. Maybe I will not be able to visit them again, but, as I am learning of the cottage, places we love we can never leave; we carry them with us.

I turn now once again to what the Rule of St Benedict has brought me, and above all to the three Benedictine vows. I want to see how they can help me to move forward at this juncture of my life. I am looking for guidance, for a set of perspectives, not law, but for an ethos, a way of life. There are three vows, which should be held in tension, each depending on and deepening the other.[70] The first is stability, the word coming from the Latin *stare*, to stand, to stand firm, earthed, grounded; then comes *conversatio morum*, which translates as conversion of manners, bringing the sense of interior transformation, being open to the new; and finally obedience, from *ob-audiens*, to listen, to listen intently, to God, to the Word, to the brothers and sisters, and above all to one's own self. All three are necessary, all uphold and strengthen me, because all three point me towards the figure of Christ.

Stability comes first; it is the cornerstone of the monastic life, as I want it to be of my own life. It is like the theme song, the underlying thread in the beautiful tapestry that St Benedict has woven for us. Although it is particularly associated with St Benedict the idea of stability has a long history within the monastic tradition, and of course in biblical understanding. The idea of steadfastness runs throughout the psalms. 'Renew a steadfast spirit within me.' One of the favourite sayings of the Desert Fathers and Mothers was 'stay in your cell and your cell will teach you everything'. There is nothing abstract here, it is thoroughly practical and down to earth. We can think of stability as sitting still, in the confidence that God in Christ sits still with us. Nothing is simpler and yet more profound than this: to remain in one place until whatever God has in store for us emerges. I am now in a new place and this applies to me – to stay still, trying to root myself here, and simply wait. St Benedict as always shows a shrewd grasp of the human psyche. To live by stability teaches me to live with myself, to come to know myself, and to resist the temptation to run away, in whatever form that might take, not least escapist daydreams, or the longing to be somewhere else. Above all it is a shield against self-deception, for it brings self-knowledge. Then if I am at home with myself I am better able to establish firm relationships with others. In the monastery this means with those with whom one would have to live for a lifetime – the irritation of a monk in choir singing off-key, the irritation of a sister who always slurps her soup. I think in my case, living now in a large complex of apartments, that will mean respecting the otherness of the other and being willing to show tolerance.[71]

Conversatio morum – the translation is fidelity to monastic life. Faithfulness, commitment to life wherever it might lead, or whatever might open up in the course of life's journey. I hold on to stability but I must not be static. Here is the paradox. There must be a holding together here, for without it there is no hope of moving on. I must be prepared for the process of continual transformation in which God is bringing the new out of the old. 'I will give you a new heart and put a new spirit within you.' Here the implication is of journeying on, of looking forward even though it may well be a daily struggle. Sometimes it seems only possible to take one small step at a time. Nevertheless, it is vital. It is just a matter of somehow keeping on keeping on, a continual bending one's life back to God whatever happens. We have no better example of how the two vows depend on one another than in Thomas Merton's life. It was because he knew that he had come home when he made his monastic commitment to the community of Gethsemani that he was able to set out both on his interior journey and then finally on his journey to the East. There he is in Bangkok on the morning of 10 December 1968 (a day that we know was to end with his sudden death) – he chose to talk about the vow of *conversatio morum*. He said that it was the most mysterious of all the vows, but

> when you stop and think about it ... the most essential. I believe that it can be interpreted as a commitment to total inner transformation of one sort or another – a commitment to become a completely new man, new woman. It seems to me that that could be regarded as the end of the monastic life, and that no matter where one attempts to do this, that remains the essential thing.

The question that underlies the Benedictine life – the question that I should be asking myself daily – is quite simply, 'Am I becoming a more loving person?' The life that St Benedict lays before me is a dynamic movement centred upon Christ. 'Are you hastening towards your heavenly home?' There is urgency in the words he chooses, he is telling me to run not walk.

The Latin root of the third of the vows helps me to rid myself of any idea that this is prompt, unquestioning, automatic obedience to some superior. It is a far deeper concept. *Ob-audiens* means listening, listening intently, 'with the ear of the heart', as St Benedict puts it in the Prologue. 'Listen' is everywhere in the Bible, particularly from the prophets arresting attention by crying: 'Listen to my voice; then I will be your God and you shall be my people. Walk exactly in the way I command you, so that you may prosper' (Jeremiah 7.22–23). One might say that the whole of the Rule is about listening – right from the start in its opening words: 'Listen carefully, my son ...' Every member of a monastic community, as also each one of us, is addressed as the prodigal who first lost himself in his own pursuits, and then came to himself, listening to the voice of his Father calling him home. It means a letting go of illusion and false goals, of all the things that had become idols, and instead hearing the voice of God in his heart – and responding to that. I can remember Dom Daniel Rees, the prior of Downside, saying that obedience is not a discipline but a mystery at the heart of redemption and of Christian life. We have only to think of Christ in the garden of Gethsemane to see how costly it is to listen to the will of the Father, and make a free response.

All three vows are necessary, they are interdependent, and each supports and upholds the other. Each has played an important role in my life – they have become guide-posts helping me to find the right direction, a point of reference particularly at times of decision. Stability, staying power, is foundational. The commitment to continual transformation is essential – I must change and journey on, whatever the cost. These two vows have shown me much about myself – they reflect St Benedict's grasp of how the psyche works best. Here is good, sound wisdom. But if that were all I would simply be in the hands of a good psychologist. If I am to listen, then that changes the perspective. I must listen and respond, to others, to the circumstances of daily life, but above all listen and obey the voice of Christ.

All three vows are necessary. And all three point me to the figure of Christ.

Stability: Christ, the Rock on whom I build.
Conversatio morum: Christ, the Way I follow.
Obedience: Christ, the Word I hear.

The Interior Space

There is so much time to be alone in this new situation. There is an absence of familiar birds and of the small creatures that congregated around the cottage. I no longer have the moon and the stars for company. I miss my neighbours at the bottom of the valley. All this makes me think about what I want to call my inner sanctuary, the void at the heart of my being, the space that I try to keep free and empty. Sadly it is far too often 'a room that many people spend a lifetime not entering',[72] in the words of the Cistercian Erik Varden. It can best be spoken of in images. St Augustine says that we need 'the Sabbath in the heart'. Hugh of St Victor in the twelfth century has a flood of images:

Now, therefore, enter your own inmost heart, and make a dwelling place for God ... Make him an ark of the covenant, make him an ark of the flood; no matter what you call it, it is all one house of God ... God is become everything to you, and God has made everything for you. He has made the dwelling, and is become your refuge.[73]

Although our circumstances could hardly be more unalike, I identify with Esther (Etty) Hillesum, the young Jewish woman born in Holland in 1914, who shows us in her letters and journal just how strong was her sense of God's dwelling place inside her – strong enough to support her even in the transit camp at Westerbork, and finally on the train to Auschwitz where she was to die in November 1943. She writes describing it in different terms: at one time it may be 'a vast empty plain, with none of the treacherous undergrowth to impede the view, so that something of "God" can enter you, and something of "Love" too'.[74] A little later she says: 'There is a really deep well inside me. And in it dwells God. Sometimes I am there too. But more often stones and grit block the well, and God is buried beneath. Then He must be dug out.' Her struggle is to 'safeguard that little piece of You, God, in ourselves'.[75] But most frequently she writes of the silent space that she carries within her, and how she would spend time sitting in it. 'There is a vast silence within me that continues to grow.' It was this that brought her the inner strength when the externals of her life were, as she confessed, quite appalling, and at the transit camp she witnessed many atrocities. She is exhausted, and yet she can still say: 'You have made me so rich, O God, please let me share out Your beauty with open hands. My life has become an uninterrupted dialogue with You, O God, one great dialogue.' This brought her a kind of joy, so that she would walk with a spring in her step feeling that life was glorious.

In almost the last letter that we have from her she insisted that she was fine, reading the psalms, studying Russian and talking to old women about their lives. 'We hardly realize it ourselves: we have become marked by suffering. And yet life in its unfathomable depths is so wonderfully good, Maria – I have to come back to that time and again.'[76] On 7 September, as she left, with her family, for the three-day rail journey to Auschwitz, she wrote a card that she threw out of the train, and which was picked up and mailed back to Holland. 'Opening the Bible at random I find this: "the Lord is my high tower". I am sitting on my rucksack in the middle of a full freight car. We left the camp singing.'[77] She died a few days later. We cannot of course know what it was that she was reading but I like to think that it might have been Psalm 18 where the images of God as a stronghold come tumbling out:

I love you, Lord, my strength,
my rock, my fortress, my saviour.
My God is the rock where I take refuge;
my shield, my mighty help, my stronghold.

Trying to punctuate a day by times of silence and prayer brings a scaffolding, a structure, which is just what I need in a time of uncertainty and transition. It helps me to live one day at a time, more consciously and responsively – and that after all is sometimes all that I can manage. Even though I do not say the office of Vigils I know that it is there, at the start of the day, a reminder about being vigilant, becoming aware and attentive to the coming of the dawn, to the coming of Christ. Then at the end of each day there is the time of handing over the day in preparation for the night's sleep with the saying of Compline, to make the day complete. And in the middle of the day, with the sun high in the sky, comes the short pause for noonday prayer. This was the time for the Desert Mothers and Fathers of *accidie*, 'the pestilence that stalks in the noonday' (Psalm 91), what they called the noonday demon, spiritual list-lessness, when the temptation was to think that if they were elsewhere all would be well. Noonday prayer is very brief, made up of short prayers and no canticle. But for the other offices, Mattins and Evensong, in addition to the psalms which change daily, there are also the three biblical canticles, which have an important role to play in the creative handling of time. They remain constant, and so I come to know them well. In the morning it is the song of the old man Zechariah, the canticle which is forward-looking, full of promise, words that I say daily and that sing in the heart:

> By the tender mercy of our God
>> the dawn from on high will break upon us.

The evening time of prayer is celebrated by Vespers or Evensong, where we say the Magnificat, the song of Mary: 'His mercy is from age to age.' Mary remembers the prom-ises of the Lord, she recounts his great deeds, for it is only with that memory that she can live this strange present moment of her mysterious pregnancy and face an unknown future with confidence. And finally with Compline comes the ending of the day, when I am given prayers that will make the day complete. The song is that of the old man Simeon: 'Lord, lettest thou thy servant depart in peace ...' He has waited and waited, and now at last he can let go, let go into sleep, let go into death.

At last, all-powerful Master,
you give leave to your servant,
to go in peace, according to your promise.

So I too must let go of the day if I am to sleep; I must
surrender control and hand over everything into the
loving hands of God. How vital this is if I am learning to
live each day well. The morning voice of God summoned
me to the new, and then throughout the day there has
been the assurance of the protecting, supporting presence
of God surrounding me with merciful love, until at the end
comes this final song of trust in that ever present mercy of
God.

The Mercy

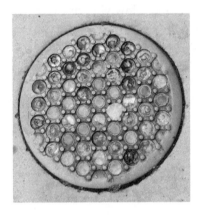

Thomas Merton writes vividly of what that mercy meant to him. These are his hermitage years, having left the monastery for a breeze-block hut in the woods nearby. He is now living and praying on his own. What that was like we know from the small book *Day of a Stranger*, which he illustrated with his own photographs. He began each day before dawn when he said that he had a large darkness and a small room of radiance with psalms in it. By this time, the year is 1965, he will have been praying daily in choir with his brothers in the monastery for more than twenty years. We can see what the psalms have come to mean for him:

> The psalms grow up silently by themselves without effort like plants in this light which is favorable to them. The

plants hold themselves up on stems which have a single consistency, that of mercy, or rather great mercy. *Magna Misericordia*. In the formlessness of night and silence a word then pronounces itself: Mercy.[78]

Merton had written of mercy before in a most memorable passage which comes at the end of his meditation 'Firewatch' in his *Sign of Jonas*. The voice of God is speaking: 'Mercy upon mercy upon mercy ...' Perhaps he was unconsciously echoing the words with which St Benedict had ended his chapter on the tools for good works: 'And finally, never lose hope in God's mercy.'

Mercy, *or hesed* in Hebrew, loving kindness, runs like an undercurrent throughout the Bible and the Fathers; it is a theme song of the psalms:

The utter mercy of God:
    Enfold me in your love, dear God,
    Yet pierce my heart with your mercy.[79]

I want to explore this concept of mercy as the undeserved love, relentlessly being poured out by God. There are those familiar lines from the prophet Micah where prophecy becomes poetry: 'and what doth the Lord require of thee, but to do justly, and to love mercy, and to walk humbly with thy God?' (6.8). Mercy appears in both those canticles so it is something that we recall daily. And then the Te Deum, sung on feast days, ends its glorious long shout of praise: 'Have mercy on us, Lord, have mercy. May your mercy always be with us, Lord/ for we have hoped in you.' There is hope and there is promise, for the one sure thing is the certainty of God's promise. 'Dearly beloved' says Pope Leo in one of his letters, 'the earth is always filled with the Mercy of the Lord.'

Whenever we say *Kyrie eleison*, Lord have mercy, we come near to the heart of its meaning, for the Greek word for mercy, *eleison*, has the same root as the word for oil, *eleon*. So mercy can be seen like oil being poured into the wounds of a suffering world, a suffering person, in need of healing. Helen Luke gives us an interesting (though rather whimsical) interpretation of the mercy. In its origin she says it is connected to commerce, to merchandise and thus to images of exchange – the French 'merci', thank you, is a grateful response. But then she takes us a step further, to compassion and forgiveness, by which we are able to open up ourselves to the Mercy. And that is the ultimate exchange. The choice is ours. God gives us the freedom to choose. She calls it God's courtesy: 'We may say "yes" to forgiveness and pierce to Mercy or say "no" and choose imprisonment.'[80]

In a short story by Flannery O'Connor, Mr Head takes his young grandson to the city, determined to make it a day that will ensure that he never wants to return. At one point they get hopelessly lost, then they fall out, and finally they find themselves in a prosperous white suburb. Here they see the plaster figure of a black man, at the end of a garden, holding a piece of watermelon. They gaze at this figure as if they were faced by some great mystery, and they could both 'feel it dissolving their differences like an action of mercy. Mr Head had never known before what mercy felt like ... but he felt he knew now.' Later on, when they manage to get back home, he stood very still and felt the action of mercy touch him, but this time he knew that there were no words in the world that could name it;

He stood appalled, judging himself with the thorough-ness of God, while the action of mercy covered his pride like a flame and consumed it … He realized that he was forgiven for sins from the beginning of time … and since God loved in proportion as He forgave, he felt ready at that instant to enter Paradise.

Mr Head realizes that he is forgiven and that he can forgive himself. It is a profound moment.[81]

Forgiveness

Increasingly over the years I have come to recognize the extent to which forgiving is about letting go – after all, the Greek that we translate as forgive, *aphiemi*, means to let go. Perhaps I am hanging on to hurt and grievance, the suffering that brings me the status of victim. Yet every time that I say the Lord's Prayer I am being given the chance to say yes to forgiveness. It is only too easy, however, to let familiarity with those words dull the enormous significance of what I am saying. Two clauses deal with forgiveness: forgiveness of my own self; my forgiveness of those who have sinned against me. These clauses come after we have asked for our daily bread. So our need to forgive and to be forgiven is on a par with our daily need to eat. It is the only obligation in the Lord's Prayer. When St Benedict decreed that the Lord's Prayer be said twice a day he knew the vital importance of the daily need to repair and renew broken relationships, and the danger of hanging on to unhealed hurts and grievances.

Letting go of the past, its injuries and injustices, can be hard – partly because I cherish them, keep their memory alive. The past was not without its faults, and I was implicated in them; but the past is past and nothing can change that. How I choose to remember is in my power. I can decide what lens I place over the persons and the events that have caused me so much pain. For hanging on to hatred, or to dreams of revenge, can hurt me more than the original occasion. The status of the righteous injured can become attractive. But I must let my adversary go free – into freedom; I do not dictate the terms under which I would want them to now live. And then there is real freedom for myself. I am liberated! Failure to forgive freezes one in the past.[82] I may have to forgive time and time again. But when I forgive I set a prisoner free and discover that the prisoner whom I set free is my own self. For I am the recipient of forgiveness, unconditional, endless forgiveness. The prodigal had no time to offer his plea of repentance. A loving, compassionate father embraces him, rushing forward to greet him. Christ on the cross, a suffering, naked figure, forgives those who are crucifying him. Could anything demonstrate more fully the power of forgiveness?

So much of Jesus' teaching in the Gospels is, in some way or another, about forgiveness. 'Neither do I condemn you.' The scene in which Jesus uttered these words is a dramatic one as it is told in chapter 8 of St John's Gospel. We are being given a succinct expression of the mercy of Jesus, Raymond Brown tells us, as he elucidates the meaning of what he calls one of the great gospel lessons. It shows the delicate balance between the justice of Jesus in not condoning the sin and his mercy in forgiving the sinner. The men had gathered round the woman taken in adultery, picking up stones, ready to stone her, an action which will take the spotlight off themselves. Then Jesus speaks: 'Let him who is without sin throw the first stone.' The men put down their stones and leave, and Jesus speaks to the woman in terms that tell her that she is accepted. She is severed, cut free from her past, free to go away, free to make a new life.[83]

The Prodigal Son

I come back time and again to the story of the prodigal son. It might well be renamed the story of the lost son, or the story of the compassionate and forgiving father. It tells us so much about the generosity and the unconditional love that lies at the heart of forgiveness. Although – like the Lord's Prayer – it is very familiar, yet we can still return to it and retell it time and again. Henri Nowen went to Leningrad specially to see the original Rembrandt painting and spent days there looking at it. He in turn helps us in his book *The Return of the Prodigal Son*[84] to see afresh the half-blind old man, with a rather rough beard, dressed in an embroidered garment below a red cloak, his two hands resting on the shoulders of his son, whose shaven head touches his breast. The son is wearing a torn yellow-brown undergarment without any cloak. His left foot has slipped from the worn sandal, and is grazed and bleeding. Yet, and Henri Nouwen draws our attention to this small but significant detail, he has his sword, the only remaining sign of dignity – he has clung to this symbol of his sonship despite his deprivation and degradation. He has come a long way, both literally and metaphorically; he has squandered his inheritance. Driven by starvation he returns, not expecting anything more than a servant's status. But the father rushes out to meet him, and without waiting for any confession or guilt-ridden apology, he kisses him and places his hands in blessing on the son's shoulders. Those two hands are interesting: the right hand is gentle, almost making a caressing movement; the left is firm and strong, as though instilling strength. Profoundly moved by the picture, Henri Nouwen said that looking at it had brought him a whole new interior understanding of tenderness, mercy and forgiveness. Seldom has God's immense, compassionate love been expressed in a more poignant way. Everything in the posture, the facial expression, the hands, speak of the divine love for humanity.

And now in the gospel story the father brings him home and clothes him in the best robe: in Greek, 'the first robe'.[85] The early theologians saw here a reference to the first robe that Adam wore before the fall. However we choose to interpret it, it is clearly a ritual release of the son from shame. For Henri Nouwen it is 'the end of the great rebellion'. The rebellion of Adam and all his descendants is forgiven, and the original blessing by which Adam received everlasting life is restored. Then follows the feasting. Not only has the father been spontaneous in rushing out to greet his son (and thereby we imagine throwing dignity to the winds), now he wants to share with him the riches of the household in the shape of music and dancing. Meanwhile, in Rembrandt's depiction, we see the elder brother standing on the outside of the circle, sulking, unforgiving, doubtless mulling over in his mind his grievances: 'For all these years I have worked like a slave for you ... yet you have never given me even a young goat to celebrate ... yet this son of yours comes home and you kill the fatted calf.' The tragedy is that the circle from which he is so deliberately determined to withhold himself is not simply jollity but 'the vast joy that is the life of God, large enough to gather all sorrow and transcend it ... It is more than an emotion. It is God's own life.'[86]

We have only to ask. When I go back to the old Irish litanies I find that they appeal for forgiveness again and again, crying out to God, addressing him by every name and every attribute: O true Physician; O Friend; O Heart-pitier; O Bestower of every treasure. These are the private prayers of an ancient people, and they touch me at a very deep, primal level, full of images drawn from early Celtic tradition. They bring the totality of their world view into play: O only life of all created things, O only light of the seven heavens. O true friend. And then simply the word, 'Forgive'. That is all that there is to say. God knows the rest. 'A Litany of Jesus' is wonderfully warm and vibrant:

O holy Jesu:
O gentle friend;
O morning star;
O mid-day Sun adorned;
O brilliant flame of the righteous and of everlasting life,
    and of eternity;
O Fountain ever-new, ever-living, ever-lasting;
O true and loving brother;
O clement and friendly one;
Forgive.[87]

The process of forgiveness can take time, it is complex and nuanced, it may mean many small steps. In my mind I picture it as being like crossing a river on a path of stepping stones, some more secure than others; some which have no firm base are quite perilous, others are well settled and offer safe passage, giving me a moment where I can pause. I have to make the crossing step by step, steadily and carefully. Anyone with any sense having to make a crossing like this would take a stout staff – I picture the figure of Christ alongside me on whom I can depend. How vital it is not to postpone setting out on this crossing. 'If we die leaving our brother, daughter, friend with the wrong they have done us unforgiven, not only are they left with this burden to carry forward for as long as they live, we also leave them the knife-edge of our rancour to twist in the wound.' And that, as Pauline Matarasso says, is exerting a form of control beyond the grave.[88]

The words of Christ from the cross show that there are no limits to forgiveness. It sometimes seems that in today's world there are happenings so terrible that they cannot be either forgotten or forgiven. Yet we have the example of Dom Christian de Chergé, the prior of the Trappist Monastère Notre Dame de l'Atlas in Tibhirine, Algeria, to show that this need not be so. This small group of seven men knew that their lives were in danger from the Groupe Islamiste Armé, yet they refused to leave their monastery, for they wished to be a sign of peace. This testament was written in December 1993, and renewed on 1 January 1994, just a few days after the monks were visited by the armed group who would later take their lives. The testament was opened on Pentecost Sunday 1996. It was written in case Christian de Chergé should become a victim of terrorism:

I should like, when the time comes, to have a space of
    lucidity
which would enable me to beg forgiveness of God
and of my brother human beings,
and at the same time to forgive with all my heart the
    one who would strike me down.
...
In this THANK YOU, which is said for everything in
    my life, from now on,
I certainly include you, friends of yesterday and today,
and you, O my friends of this place,
besides my mother and father, my sisters and brothers
    and their families,
a hundredfold as was promised!
And you, too, my last minute friend, who would not
    have known what you are doing.
Yes, for you too I say this THANK YOU and this
    A-DIEU – to commend you to the God in whose face
    I see yours.
And may we find each other, happy 'good thieves' in
    Paradise,
if it please God, the Father of us both. AMEN![89]

'Our Christian identity is always in the process of being
born. It is a Paschal identity.' Fr Christian de Chergé was
addressing the general chapter of the Cistercians in 1993.[90]
What joyous and yet challenging news this is! Every con-
tact with Christ is Easter. We should all be able to put on
the risen Christ, just as we should be able to see the resur-
rected face of the Easter Christ in the face of others. 'Let
everyone who comes be received as Christ.' St Benedict
said this in connection with hospitality and the welcome
given to guests, but the principle applies to all comers.
He is, as always, writing out of his own experience. In

the cave at Subiaco where he has been living alone and in silence, when a priest comes to greet him on Easter day, St Benedict exclaimed: 'Easter indeed, brother, it is since you are here.' He sees Easter in the other. And if this is the reality of our lives we might also hope to keep in our hearts that deep, inward joy which is paschal joy.

Diminishment

The American Franciscan Richard Rohr often speaks of a spirituality of subtraction, a phrase which jars with me – nevertheless, if it encourages me to think of how that applies in my own life it can then become a useful exercise. I know that I have to let go as I age, for otherwise I shall be clinging to the past, and that will prevent the new, in whatever form that might take, from coming to birth. Letting go has a hidden freedom in it, for surrendering is really a liberation, allowing me to live fully but differently. I notice that I am walking more slowly, whereas I used to stride; I find that I cannot read easily without glasses, whereas I used to be proud of my sight; and worst of all, I am becoming forgetful. I have to face that fact, the price I pay as I am growing older. The time has come when the questions which I might have asked at earlier stages of my life about my identity, and about sharing with God in the creation of that identity, now become more urgent. Helen

Luke sets out quite starkly the choice that lies ahead in old age. We may continue to cling to our past achievements or we may, in Shakespeare's words, 'take upon the mystery of things, as if we were God's spies'.[91] A spy of God is one who penetrates into a hidden mystery – one who finds the most trivial of things touched by wonder. Getting older makes me aware how amazing it is to have been alive in the first place! Time is different in old age: 'time on our hands' becomes a common expression. Thinking about it, I picture my hands as wide open for this precious gift of more time than I have had in previous years. Increasingly I find that poetry is now the best language, because it has to be read and reread slowly. It is a vehicle for seeing things anew, as if for the first time. I can remember Gillian Clarke (then the poet laureate of Wales) saying in a talk at the Hay Literary Festival that a good poem stops you dead in your tracks, as if you saw the burning bush.

At one level I am no longer 'living life to the full', and yet if my days are numbered time becomes precious, unrepeatable. I want to live each moment with greater intensity. Life now brings a greater opportunity to pay attention, to look consciously at the ordinary minutiae of daily life in the things around – in the words of Helen Luke, seeing the most trivial of things touched by wonder. I carry a magnifying glass, and use it for looking at such things as lichen, which I might otherwise so easily pass by. In earlier days I would use a camera to take photographs in order to *record* – family life, holidays, significant events – but now as I take my camera with me on my daily walk I think of it as an instrument of contemplation and amazement and rejoicing. I really look at things quite intensely, so that I forget everything else.

This teaches me to make the distinction between capturing or possessing and standing back in awe and delight. I try to approach reality with tenderness, as Ansel Adams, that greatest of American photographers, said – so that the photograph becomes an expression of love and of revelation. A true photograph does not need words, it does not need to be explained, it brings images of endless moments. I am looking as I walk, with an almost intuitive search for form and shape and relationship, and thus for meaning. It brings an unfolding of what lies directly around me, which may not be the perfect rose or the perfect sunrise, but may still be able to startle me, become the occasion for amazement. This will escape me unless I am totally present. And then the mystery is that something that I have seen becomes an image which years later says something totally other. It takes time for a thing to communicate its self, its essence. I notice pattern and texture, I notice light and shadow. I pick up a snail shell, a twig, a feather. I look at the underside of a leaf. Walking along the Thames I am aware of the reflections of the water and the jubilance of the light. Walking the city streets I look at the patterns on drain covers, the decoration on mailboxes, details of street furniture to which the milling crowd of people around me seem oblivious. Taking a photograph makes me walk slowly. I become willing to wait, accepting what lies around me – it helps me to put down roots in a new environment. Perhaps as I grow older my whole world will shrink – to a room in a care home, to a hospital ward – and then will come the time of further testing. Will I be able to hold on to that sense of wonder? Will I still be able to find delight in whatever lies around me? Will I see with gratitude all that is given in a new, and possibly ultimate, situation?

'I have no time for the ageing process.' This was the stout declaration of the painter Marie Louise Motesiczky[92] in the exhibition of her work at the Tate in 2020. She said that she would paint portraits of her mother time and again with a raw honesty, without her wig, bald and decrepit, because she saw in her something beautiful – 'like someone never expelled from Paradise'. Even as a young man Rembrandt wanted to paint old age, and he did it with the same raw honesty. Furrowed brow, drooping eyelids, the heavy lines of the face, a glimpse of white hair – all the marks of ageing are there. And so it is with Rembrandt's last self-portrait, in those blood-streaked old eyes, a look of certainty of pardon.

We need art and we need storytelling to bring to us these truths about ageing. I come back to the figure of Odysseus making his final journey, carrying on his shoulder the oar that has played an essential role in his roving, adventurous past. He comes to an inland country where it is not recognized and instead is called a winnowing fan. A wayfarer and he dig a hole and the heavy oar is placed in it, at last standing upright between earth and heaven. When he is asked what the winnowing fan means to him, Odysseus replies that it makes a wind that separates the chaff from the grain at the time of harvest. Then the wayfarer tells him that now is the time of harvest and he stands in the autumn of his life. That great oar is no longer the driving force carrying him over the oceans of his outer and inner worlds but an instrument of discriminating wisdom separating, moment by moment, the wheat of life from the chaff, an instrument of knowing the difference between the essential and the non-essential. As Odysseus puts down the heavy oar that he has carried so far and as he is relieved of its weight, he realizes that this is the final letting go of everything that has hitherto given meaning to his life, a letting go of all human endeavours, activity, achievements. He can go home to Penelope; he is free now to let his life ebb gently away.[93]

A photo falls out of a book and I am startled to see my younger self, sitting in a field with a straw basket beside me, my hands clasped round my knees. It would have been taken just before my wedding, sixty years ago. The long black hair is white now, the hands wrinkled with mottled spots, the face lined. I am at the stage of life when many of the things that I used to do are past. I can no longer walk great distances or climb a hill. And I have to give up many of my dreams of things that I had hoped to do, places that I longed to see. I try to accept diminishment and try to do it willingly and without a grudge. Teilhard de Chardin spoke of the erosions of age, and how they leave their marks on both body and mind. It is a word that I like, for it suggests a crumbling, a wearing away. Another metaphor is to describe it as a process of pruning and I suppose that that is one way of looking at it – cutting back so that fruitfulness may grow. I find that both apply at different times. But whatever the pattern, I hope that God is going to work within my limitations. I need now more than ever to be at home in myself. Diminishment brings an invitation to become more contemplative, to carry a heart of silence, to resist the temptation to immediately fill up the precious emptiness.

Death can no longer be something remote; these are the years that I am awaiting death. This is the one certainty that we all have. I have reached the fourscore years that the psalmist speaks of and there he tells me to expect labour and sorrow (Psalm 90). As I think how I am going to face these coming years I turn to fortitude. It is one of the four cardinal virtues, traceable back to the Stoics – and beyond that probably to Socrates. I claim it because unlike the other three (prudence, justice and temperance) it has more to do with character than with conduct, it is a quality that I can nurture. It has many of the qualities that

I associate with the ancient oak beside the cottage gate – stability, rootedness, strength. It is a safeguard against the self-pity that can all too easily become so attractive and so insidious. I want to prepare for the years ahead that almost inevitably will bring some form of suffering. There will be the physical diminishments, the loss of memory, or of sight or hearing, the restrictions that a frail body will impose. There will be damage to the fabric of myself that cannot be repaired. And above all there will be times when I feel huge sadness, washing over me like a great wave, when I realize that my life will disappear and I shall not be there to see how my family are living, how my children and my grandchildren are growing, and how they will be in a world that I cannot begin to imagine. This will be the final letting go.

Death

Today many people seem to hesitate to talk about death and dying easily and unselfconsciously – we even hesitate to use the word itself and instead say 'passed'. If death is taboo, or at least uncomfortable, in daily life and conversation, then poetry and music have no scruples: they both confront grief and loss. My own hope when it comes to the hour of my death is to be able to say: 'My roots are deep in eternity.' I take heart from those standing on the edge of death who yet speak of it positively. There is the well-known instance of Dietrich Bonhoeffer whispering his final message to a fellow prisoner in 1945 as he was being taken away to be executed: 'This is the end, but for me the beginning' – a message which reached his friend Bishop George Bell in London.

Etty Hillesum on her way to the death camp looked

death in the face, no longer wasting energy on fear of death, or refusing to acknowledge its inevitability, full of life to the last.

Death and life are interwoven in the night chants and prayers of the *Carmina Gadelica* – here are a people who thought entirely naturally about death. They felt themselves surrounded by the members of the Trinity, by saints and angels, by day and by night, 'from the top of my face to the edge of my soles', as one old woman put it. Living with this assurance, the thought of death was a natural part of life. Going to bed each night carried a bed-blessing:

> I lie in my bed tonight
> As I would lie in the grave,
> Thine arm beneath my neck,
> Thou son of Mary victorious.

> Angels shall watch me
> And I lying in slumber,
> And angels shall guard me
> In the sleep of the grave.

For them it was difficult to think of sleep without thinking of death, and impossible to think of either except in terms of the continuing presence of the victorious Christ. Death is part of life, death is not feared:

> I am lying down to-night as beseems
> In the fellowship of Christ, Son of the Virgin of ringlets.
> In the fellowship of the gracious Father of glory.
> In the fellowship of the Spirit of powerful aid.
> I am lying down to-night with God,
> And God to-night will lie down with me.

They address God with both intimacy and awe: they pray to Christ as shepherd and herdsman, someone who understands their way of life, but they also acclaim him as Paschal Son and Son of the tears, of the wounds, of the piercings. They carried with them in life and in death the assurance that the will of God would not lead them where the love of God could not reach them. There is profound consolation here as life is ebbing away. There is one blessing that was clearly used for someone close to death, which has a wonderful immediacy about it, as I found when I used it at the bedside of an old sister who was dying in a convent in Wales:

> Be each saint in heaven,
> Each sainted woman in heaven,
> Each angel in heaven
> Stretching their arms for you,
> Smoothing the way for you,
> When you go thither
>   Over the river hard to see;
> Oh when you go thither home
>   Over the river hard to see.[94]

Death was for St Benedict a natural thing, and he told his followers: 'Day by day remind yourself that you are going to die' (4.v.47). It reads better in the Latin: *mortem cotidie ante oculos suspectam habere*. It remains a stark statement. I well remember the way in which it was expressed in a Trappist monastery in Snowmass in the United States. Behind the altar on the east wall of the chapel there hung a very simple wooden cross, which would stay there until it was taken down to mark the grave of the next brother to die. So death was a very natural part of daily life. That simple cross has remained very powerfully in my mind, as all good images should. It illustrates those words from the Rule. Chapter 4, from which this verse is taken, is often called 'The Tools of Good Works', and it is a compendium of short commandments, aphorisms, biblical quotations. If read in isolation St Benedict's injunction might sound threatening, negative, far removed from the voice of love and energy that permeates the Prologue. But putting it into context brings a different connotation. Earlier on he has told us that keeping any of these precepts will be impossible if we are going to be self-reliant. We must put our trust in God and admit our total dependence on him: 'Place your hope in God alone' (v. 41). Verse 46, immediately preceding the admonition about death, says: 'Yearn for everlasting life with holy desire.' And then in the two verses that follow: 'Hour by hour keep careful watch over all you do, aware that God's gaze is upon you, wherever you may be.' St Benedict is shaping our attitude, educating our approach. As the hour of death approaches we are to await it with trust and hope; hope and fear cannot co-exist, our God is trustworthy. How much that promise of hope is a theme of the psalms! Here is the prayer with which Jim Cotter ends Psalm 90, bringing out that perspective:

Eternal God,
thank you for your gift of time and the measure death
    gives to our days.
They pass so quickly as to dent our pride.
May we neither rely on our achievements nor be
    downcast at our failures.
Keep us but faithful to your love, and dependent on
    your grace alone.
We ask this in the Spirit of the One who died a human
    failure, and died so young.

The psalm is addressed to 'God of eternity; God beyond time/ our refuge and hope from one generation to another'. And throughout comes this haunting refrain: 'Amidst the confusions of time, may we hear eternity's heartbeat.'

From dust we came, from dust we return.
'Be shaped from clay, be crumbled to earth.'
Creator of life, of death, so did you order our ways.
A thousand years in your sight are as yesterday.
As a watch in the night comes quickly to an end,
so the years pass before you, in a flicker of the eye.
Amidst the confusions of time,
may we hear eternity's heartbeat.[95]

The Stations of the Cross

As the church's year moves through Passiontide and Holy Week to the day of resurrection, there comes the yearly reminder of how we too accompany Christ on that final journey of his human life, following the steps that he took on his journey to Golgotha, the place of his crucifixion. Artists and sculptors have painted and carved the stations of the cross. Those fourteen steps or stages run round the walls of many churches, often beautiful and prayer-filled, sometimes dramatic and challenging. They have caught the imagination of such sculptors as Eric Gill. But they need not be indoors – I have walked the stations on a windy hillside in South Africa, moving from wooden cross to wooden cross, accompanied by the monastery dog. They are to be found in places ranging from a church in an African township to a woodland site belonging to a retreat house. One of my dreams had been to make a pathway of fourteen stations from tree to tree at the cottage copse and orchard.

And now I am about to make this journey for myself, a ritual walk so that the fourteen stations of the way of the cross become my own way too, for at each step I am questioned by the scene before me. It is not just a journey for Jesus, it is my own story too. It starts with the dark and horrendous news: Jesus is condemned to die. He has been dragged before Pilate, his back torn with scourges, his head crowned with thorns, and he is condemned to a disgraceful death. This is stark: it does not let me forget that I shall one day die. That inescapable fact is the underlying truth of the journey that I am now making. A heavy cross is laid upon Jesus' shoulders, and he falls time and again. I picture that clumsily made cross, of splintered wood, the uneven ground, and the aching shoulders. But I think of those early Desert Mothers and Fathers who tell us that there is only the simple response, 'fall and get up again', time after time. I also must expect to take up burdens, struggle with loads heavy on my heart. From Jesus I have the example of someone who carried this burden, thinking not of himself. Then other characters appear along the way: Jesus' mother Mary, Simon of Cyrene, Veronica, some women from the crowd. A woman brings just whatever comes to hand, a scrap of cloth, not even anything whole – I think of those many people whom I have met on my journey and of what I owe to them, often not recognizing sufficiently the role that they have played in my life. Did I see Christ in them? Then when at the tenth station as Jesus is stripped of his clothes there is the act of letting go for which I need all the commitment and strength that I can summon. I can cling to nothing, everything must be given up. And then at last Jesus faces death, nailed to that disgraceful wood. It is a death of quite excruciating suffering there on that cross, and when it is all over the stone tomb receives him. And so, is that the end?

> We too, O God, will descend into the grave,
> whenever it shall please you,
> as it shall please you
> and wheresoever it shall please you.
> Let your just decrees be fulfilled;
> let our sinful bodies return to their parent dust,
> but do you, in your great mercy,
> receive our immortal souls,
> and when our bodies have risen again,
> place them likewise in your kingdom
> that we may love and bless you for ever and ever.
> Amen.[96]

The measured words of the eighteenth-century Bishop Richard Challoner, which bring to an end the stations of the cross, I make into a prayer for my own death, whenever and wheresoever that will be. I know only that it will be peculiarly and poignantly mine, and that it is a mystery, but I hold only my hope that I will be with the risen Christ.

Christ's body has been placed in the tomb and now there is the mystery of Holy Saturday, the most mysterious day of the church's calendar. It should be a day of emptiness not of busyness. It calls forth poetic language. St Ephrem, addresses Christ as the glorious son of the carpenter:

> Our Lord was trodden underfoot by death, and in turn trod upon death as upon a road ... he came to the Virgin, so that he might receive from her a chariot on which to ride to the underworld. In the body he has assumed he entered death's domain, broke open its strong-room and scattered its treasure.

And then there is the ancient homily, which opens so dramatically: 'What is happening? Today there is a great silence over the earth, and stillness, a great silence because the King sleeps.' Holding his glorious weapon, the cross, Christ goes down into the underworld, seeking to free Adam and Eve from their pains. Grasping Adam's hand he raises him up saying: 'Awake, O sleeper, and arise from the dead, and Christ shall give you light.' Then come words which although addressed to Adam speak to any one of us:

I command you: Awake, sleeper,
I have not made you to be held a prisoner in the underworld.
Arise from the dead; I am the life of the dead.
Arise, O human being, work of my hands,
arise, you were fashioned in my image.
Rise, let us go hence;
for you in me, and I in you,
together, we are one undivided person.[97]

There was a ritual in walking the stations of the cross, finding along the path fresh encounters and fresh insight into familiar truths. I hold it in tension with the ritual walk of leaving the cottage. Both of them tell me, in very different ways, that it is only by letting go, by going through tears and grief, that I can reach a place of joy and liberation. But what the experience of the stations has shown me is that the risen Christ was there alongside me all the way. Perhaps I was unaware, like the two disciples on the road to Emmaus, trudging with downcast eyes, all hope gone, saying, 'We had hoped' – such poignant words. And then over a meal their eyes are opened, they realize who the stranger is, and they react with astonished amazement. In his painting in the National Gallery in London, Caravaggio shows us one disciple with arms flung wide open, the other leaping up from his chair, gestures of startled amazement.

There is another moment of amazement when Mary is startled in a garden. And then comes the words, as she is tempted to hold on to the risen Christ: 'Noli me tangere' – not, 'Do not touch' (for touching is good), but, 'Do not cling'. Here again is the message: letting go, refusing to cling to the past, is an essential step into living fully and happily in the present, and moving into an unknown future. We watch Christ who, in the Gospels, in dismissing certainties, shows us what certainties mean. He dissolves an existing situation, he challenges people to leave their nets, to leave a nice, safe booth. 'Come', he says to Peter, James and John, and Matthew. Our God is a God who moves, and he expects us to move with him. For still our God is a God of surprises – as Abraham discovered in his old age:

He was seventy-five years old
and God's first word to him
was 'Go'.

I think of Abram
when my plans go awry,
when happenstance

pries my fingers loose
from the grasping illusion
of control over life.

'Go', God said to Abram,
giving no address,
disclosing no destination.

Taking an unruly family,
trusting God to show the way,
Abram went.

On that wild journey
he, too, had fingers pried loose,
heard Sarai laugh, learned

the blessing comes
in the going
and the letting go.[98]

So we all must be prepared for a very peculiar sort of journeying – not the unfolding of foreordained, necessary patterns, but the tracing of all the diverse and unexpected factors that make things go this way rather than that. It is a journey in which growth always means one step beyond what is familiar. It is a journey which asks of me the art of letting go. God is not to be contained in a landscape, familiar and comfortable. After all, being at home is not a matter of settling down for good, in a place beyond questions or growing; it is something to do with a fundamental trust in the Christ who accompanies us in our travelling, who has been alongside us all the way.

Christ is there in the new landscape.
Home is Christ's company.
The journey of my life is one where, one by one,
I learn to let go of the things that I thought so
    important,
until at last there is only Christ.[99]

* * *

To the one that overcometh ...
Will I give a white stone
and in the stone a new name written.
(Revelation 2.17)

Notes

1 James Morris, *Oxford*, London, Faber and Faber, 1965, p. 216.

2 Bob Blaisdell, ed., *Selected Poems of Gerard Manley Hopkins*, New York, Dover Publications, Inc., 2011, p. 34.

3 There are many editions of *Jude the Obscure*; this comes at the end of Chapter 3.

4 Leonard Woolf, *Beginning Again: An Autobiography of the Years 1911–1918*, London, Harcourt Brace Jovanovich, 1975.

5 Leonard Woolf, *Downhill All the Way: An Autobiography of the Years 1919–1939*, London, Hogarth, 1967.

6 For a fascinating study, see Kate Kennedy and Hermione Lee, eds, *Lives of Houses*, Princeton and Oxford, Princeton University Press, 2020.

7 May Sarton, 'The Work of Happiness', *Collected Poems 1930–1993*, New York, W. W. Norton & Co., 1993.

8 Christian Bobin, *The Eighth Day: Key to an Open Door, Selected Writings of Christian Bobin*, ed. and trans. Pauline Matarasso, London, Darton, Longman & Todd, 2015, p. 115.

9 Gaston Bachelard, *The Poetics of Space: The Classic Look at How We Experience Intimate Places*, trans. Maria Jolas, with a new Foreword by John Stilgoe, first published in France 1958, Boston, Beacon Press, 1992.

10 See for example John Inge, *A Christian Theology of Place*, Aldershot, Ashgate, 2003.

11 See Timothy Radcliffe, *Alive in God: A Christian Imagination*, London, Bloomsbury Continuum, 2019, p. 202.

12 Quoted in Catharine Raudvere, ed., *Nostalgia, Loss and Creativity in South East Europe*, Switzerland, Palgrave Macmillan, 2018, p. 23.

13 Penelope Fitzgerald, *The Blue Flower*, London, Fourth Estate, 2013, p. 248.

14 William Fiennes, *The Music Room*, London, Picador, 2009, pp. 154–5.

15 William Fiennes, *The Music Room*, p. 131.

16 Marilynne Robinson, *Home*, London, Virago, 2008, p. 263.

17 Renée Hirschon, 'Enduring Bonds of Place: Personhood and the Loss of Home', in Raudvere, *Nostalgia, Loss and Creativity in South East Europe*, p. 23.

18 This is one of the best preserved pieces of medieval stained glass. It is the work of the Methusalah Master who came to the cathedral after the great fire of 1174. Adam is wearing a fleece loin-cloth that allows us to see the strong muscles of his arms and legs.

19 A. E. Housman, *A Shropshire Lad*, London, George G. Harrap, 1940, p. 9.

20 Philip Toynbee, *Part of a Journey: An Autobiographical Journal 1977–79*, London, Collins, Fount Paperback, 1981, p. 147.

21 Christian Bobin, *The Eighth Day*, p. 204.

22 W. Keble Martin, *The Concise British Flora in Colour*, London, Ebury Press and Michael Joseph, 1965.

23 I have written about this in my *Lost in Wonder: Rediscovering the Spiritual Art of Attentiveness*, Norwich, Canterbury Press, 2012.

24 I owe this quotation to Ann Wroe, *Six Facets of Light*, London, Jonathan Cape, 2016, p. 18.

25 Denise Levertov, *New Selected Poems*, ed. Paul A. Lacey, Hexham, Bloodaxe Books, 2003.

26 Denise Levertov, *New Selected Poems*, p. 52. I have short-ened the poem by omitting the two verses in which she is speaking about the red salamander, as not relevant to my situation!

27 Bonnie Thurston, *Practicing Silence: New and Selected Verses*, Brewster, MA, Paraclete Press, 2014.

28 Bruce Chatwin, *Winding Paths*, Introduction by Robert Calasso, London, Jonathan Cape, 1999, p. 19.

29 Robert MacFarlane, 'Ways of Connecting', *Cambridge Alumni Magazine 66*, pp. 18–21. This short article is expanded in Robert MacFarlane, *The Old Ways: A Journey on Foot*, London, Hamish Hamilton, 2012.

30 Marina Warner, *Fairy Tale: A Very Short Introduction*, Oxford, Oxford University Press, 2016, p. 17.

31 Paul Nash, *Outline: An Autobiography*, London, Faber and Faber, 1956, p. 139.

32 Edward Thomas, *The South Country*, London, J. M. Dent, Everyman, 1932, new edn, 1993.

33 This is from my *God Under My Roof: Celtic Songs and Blessings*, Oxford, SLG Press, new edn, 2020, p. 37. More journeying blessings appear in my *The Celtic Vision: Prayers and Blessings from the Outer Hebrides* (Selections from the *Carmina Gadelica*), London, Darton, Longman & Todd, 1988, reprinted 1997, pp. 141–57.

34 Alexandra Harris, *Weatherland: Writers and Artists under English Skies*, London, Thames & Hudson, 2015, pp. 46–9. In her fascinating book Alexandra Harris tells us that, according to legend, Pope Nicholas in the ninth century decreed that all churches in Christendom should carry a cock.

35 Jon M. Sweeney, 'Wonder and the Radical Visions of Francis of Assisi', in *Fairacres Chronicle*, Winter 2019, vol. 5, no. 2, p. 28.

36 Malcolm Guite, *Love, Remember: 40 Poems of Loss, Lament and Hope*, Norwich, Canterbury Press, 2017, p. 55.

37 Fernand Pouillon, *The Stones of the Abbey* (originally published by Editions du Seuil, 1964), trans. Edward Gillott, New York, Harcourt Brace, 1970, pp. 75–6. See pp. 40–1 in this book for more on Le Thoronet.

38 Entitled 'Your Garden – One Good Place', and dedicated to me, this first appeared in *The Merton Journal*, which explains the subtitle, which is a phrase of Thomas Merton. It appears in full in my *Living on the Border: Reflections on the Experience of Threshold*, Norwich, Canterbury Press, 2011, pp. 103–5.

39 Rowan Williams, in his book *The Way of St Benedict*, London, SPCK, 2020, refers to him as 'the great Roman Catholic writer'. He was Rector of the Ecumenical Institute of Tantur, and wrote among other books *Holiness*, New York, Seabury Press, 1981.

40 I have taken this from Edmund de Waal, *Psalm*, Gagosian in association with Ca'Foscari University of Venice, 2020, p. 22.

41 Elizabeth Chatwin and Nicholas Shakespeare, eds, *Under the Sun: The Letters of Bruce Chatwin*, London, Vintage Books, 2011, p. 509.

42 Chapter 32, 'The Tools and Goods of the Monastery'. I use the text *RB80: The Rule of St Benedict*, trans. Timothy Fry OSB, Collegeville, MN, Liturgical Press, 1981.

43 C. Day-Lewis, 'Walking Away', *Selected Poems*, London, Penguin, 1969, p. 35.

44 Esther de Waal, *God Under My Roof*, p. 37.

45 A. M. Allchin and Esther de Waal, eds, *Threshold of Light: Prayers and Praises from the Celtic Tradition*, London, Darton, Longman & Todd, 1986, p. 12 (shortened).

46 Celia Paul, *Self-Portrait*, London, Jonathan Cape, 2019, p. 7.

47 John Drury, *Music at Midnight: The Life and Poetry of George Herbert*, London, Allen Lane, 2013, p. 78.

48 John Pawson, *Minimum*, London, Phaidon Press, 1996.

49 Lucien Hervé, *The Architecture of Truth*, London, Phaidon, nd.

50 Bonnie Thurston, *A Place to Pay Attention*, Blaenau Ffestiniog, Cinnamon Press, 2015, p. 240.

51 I owe this to William Fiennes in his book *The Snow Geese*, London, Picador, 2003, pp. 174–6.

52 Renée Hirschon, 'Enduring Bonds of Place', p. 219.

53 Renée Hirschon, 'Enduring Bonds of Place', p. 33.

54 Words taken from an article by Erik Varden, a Cistercian of Mount St Bernard, *The Tablet*, 3 April 2021, p. 90.

55 'The Lamentation of the Dead', Inaugural Lecture by the Professor of Poetry in the University of Oxford, 25 October 1984, London, Anvil Press Poetry Ltd.

56 I owe this quotation to Alexandra Harris, 'Moving House', in Kennedy and Lee, *Lives of Houses*, p. 10.

57 Pauline Matarasso, in Christian Bobin, *The Eighth Day*, p. xxvii.

58 Esther de Waal, *The Celtic Vision*, p. 132.

59 May Sarton, *Collected Poems 1930–1993*.

60 The reference is to Sergei Ovsiannikov, *Journey to Freedom*, London, Bloomsbury Continuum, 2021, I have not read the book but only the review.

61 I have taken this from *The Divine Office II*, Collins, 2006, p. 569, but I added women.

62 Jim Cotter, *Out of the Silence … Into the Silence, Prayer's Daily Round*, Aberdaron, Cairns Publications, 2010, p. 141.

63 Extracts taken from *The Divine Office III*, pp. 180–1, 184–5, his discourses on the psalms.

64 *Rule of St Benedict*, Chapter 20, on reverence in prayer.

65 This interpretation was made in the *Rule of St Benedict*, in verse 28 of the Prologue. It is one for which I have been extremely grateful.

66 Roger Wagner, *The Book of Praises: Translations from the Psalms*, Norwich, Canterbury Press, 2021.

67 Jim Cotter, *Out of the Silence*, pp. 442–3

68 Thomas Merton, *On the Psalms*, Collegeville, MN, 1956, London, Sheldon Press, 1957, p. 7.

69 Henri Nouwen, *The Genesee Diary: Report from a Trappist Monastery*, New York, Doubleday, 1976, p. 100.

70 I write at length on the three vows in *A Life-Giving Way: A Contemplative Commentary on the Rule of St Benedict*, Norwich, Canterbury Press, 2013, pp. 165–79. All three are necessary; each supports and upholds me for they all speak to me of Christ.

71 Rowan Williams, in *The Way of St Benedict*, London, Bloomsbury, 2020, p. 7, claims that 'the Rule of St Benedict is, in one sense, all about stability'. He has many illuminating and useful things to say, but I am sorry that he has not put stability into context with the other two vows. Thomas Merton, for example, says that *conversatio morum* is the most essential vow.

72 Erik Varden, *The Tablet*, p. 90.

73 Christopher Howse, ed., *Comfort*, London, Continuum, 2004. Quoted in *The Tablet*.

74 See *An Interrupted Life: The Diaries of Etty Hillesum, 1941–43*, trans. Arnold J. Pomerans, London, Persephone Books, 1999, p. 33.

75 *An Interrupted Life*, p. 178.

76 *An Interrupted Life*, p. 424.

77 *An Interrupted Life*, p. 426.

78 Thomas Merton, *Day of a Stranger*, Salt Lake City, UT, Gibbs M. Smith, 1981.

79 Psalm 51, opening lines, in Jim Cotter, *Out of the Silence*, p. 165.

80 Helen M. Luke, *Old Age: Journey into Simplicity*, New York, Parabola Books, 1987, pp. 84–5.

81 Flannery O'Connor, 'The Artificial Nigger', in *The Complete Stories*, New York, Farrar, Strauss and Giroux, 1979, pp. 269–70.

82 This phrase is from Anthony Phillips, whose short book *Entering into the Mind of God*, London, SPCK, 2002, pp. 7–13, gives an illuminating insight into forgiveness.

83 My writing here has been influenced by the way in which Roger Wagner retold this in an Easter meditation for Iffley Church for Easter in 2020. The Raymond E. Brown reference is *The Gospel According to John* (i–xii), New York, Doubleday & Co., 1966, p. 337.

84 Henri J. M. Nouwen, *The Return of the Prodigal Son: A*

Meditation on Fathers, Brothers and Sons, New York, Doubleday, 1992.

85 I owe this to Timothy Radcliffe, *Alive in God*, p. 110.

86 Henri Nouwen, *The Return of the Prodigal Son*, p. 39.

87 Charles Plummer, ed., *Irish Litanies*, London, Henry Bradshaw Society, 1925.

88 Pauline Matarasso, *Clothed in Language*, Collegeville, MN, Liturgical Press, 2019, p. 102.

89 AIM, *Alliance for International Monasticism*, vol. 5, no. 2, 1996.

90 The talk was on the subject of Cistercian contemplative identity (see John W. Kiser, *The Monks of Tibherine: Faith, Love and Terror in Algeria*, New York, St Martin's Press, 2002).

91 Helen Luke, *Old Age: Journey into Simplicity*, Herndon VA, Lindisfarne Books, 2010, p. 30.

92 She is a distant cousin who has painted portraits of members of my family, my husband Victor when he was Dean of Canterbury, and my son Alexander.

93 See Helen Luke's chapter on the Odyssey in *Old Age*, pp. 1–25. Richard Rohr has a couple of pages on Odysseus in his *Falling Upward*, London, SPCK, 2012, pp. xxxii–xxxiii.

94 These prayers come from the section 'Night Prayers', Esther de Waal, *The Celtic Vision*, pp. 99–109. Many are included in Esther de Waal, *God Under my Roof*, Oxford, SLG Press, new edn, 2020.

95 Jim Cotter, *Out of the Silence*, p. 269.

96 Roman Catholic Bishop Richard Challoner (1691–1781) was Vicar Apostolic of the London district. I owe this to Fr Daniel Lloyd, priest of HolyRood, Oxford, who adapted the 'Way of the Cross' from Challoner's writings.

97 A reading from an ancient homily for Holy Saturday, taken from *The Divine Office II*, pp. 310–1.

98 Bonnie Thurston, *Practicing Silence*.

99 This final paragraph owes something to Archbishop Stephen Cottrell, reported in the *Church Times* on 17 July 2020, and to Archbishop Rowan Williams in *For All That Has Been, Thanks*, with Joan Chittister OSB, Norwich, Canterbury Press, 2010, pp. 81–93.